GOD'S MASTERPIECES

GOD'S MASTERPIECES

A selection of Bible readings and reflections

D.W. CLEVERLEY FORD

the bible reading fellowship

The Bible Reading Fellowship
Warwick House
25 Buckingham Palace Road
London SW1W 0PP

First published 1991
© BRF 1991

British Library Cataloguing in Publication Data
Cleverley Ford, D.W. (Douglas William)
    God's masterpieces.
    1. Christian life — Devotional works
    I. Title
    242.5

ISBN 0-900164-89-1

Typeset by Barnes Design + Print Group, Maidenhead, England
Printed by J.W. Arrowsmith Ltd., Bristol, England

Contents

THE NEW TESTAMENT

The Revised Standard Version of the Bible has been used for most of the passages, although the Authorized Version is used where the passages are particularly memorable for their classical literary style.

Acknowledgements

I wish to express my appreciation for the encouragement given to me by the Revd Shelagh Brown, Editor of the *New Daylight* series of the Bible Reading Fellowship's Notes, to write this book; also to Miss Barbara Hodge, a former colleague on the staff of Lambeth Palace, for making the typescript from my manuscript.

D.W. Cleverley Ford
Lingfield 1990

Introduction

When I was asked to write this book I hesitated. I am not a profes-
sional biblical scholar, but can only claim to be a Christian whose
faith has been nourished and enlivened by nothing so much as by
the Bible for some sixty years. If this is a qualification so be it.

It all began when I was fifteen in what I can only describe as
some tarred wooden sheds, erected on a desolate stretch of marsh
in the Norfolk broadlands. I had been invited there by our strictly
Protestant vicar who had used this makeshift caravan for holidays
with his sons when they were growing up. When they eventually
left home, he kept the place on as a kind of retreat for himself.

It was December when I was first invited there. A biting north-
east wind from the sea whistled across the marsh whipping up the
river. By four o'clock darkness had fallen and I sat with my host at a
table under a paraffin oil lamp. After tea he produced a Bible and
instructed me to read Matthew Chapter 5 aloud. At verse 3 he
stopped me and asked me what the kingdom of heaven was. I had
no idea. My schoolboy face was blank. 'Read on', he said, and I did
so until another question was put with the same result. In this way,
the evening continued, broken only by supper which my host
cooked over a Primus stove. My interest was captivated: I had been
caught by the Bible and I am still caught after sixty years.

From time to time when I could go down to the sheds on the
marsh my lessons continued. The programme involved being out
all day on the river in a boat, and returning after dark to sit under
the oil lamp with the New Testament on my lap. I began to obtain a
fair grasp of the teaching of Jesus, though I was repeatedly warned
that I could never properly read the New Testament until I was
acquainted with its original language — Greek. So I decided to
make up the deficiency.

My studies for a university degree took me into a very different
realm; detached and highly critical analysis of the Bible was the

norm — the kind of 'scientific approach' which can seem a little threatening to people whose knowledge of the Bible is mainly through worship or private devotion. My academic studies introduced me to complicated questions about dates and authorship and the different methods adopted to produce writings as we have them now. But studying the Bible in this way did not lead me astray as my former, more 'fundamentalist', teacher feared. The Bible does not have to be regarded as an infallible book completely without error or contradiction in order for it to be alive and true. What my studies taught me above all was that the Bible is a stunning literary masterpiece, a remarkable record of responses to, and visions of, the sacred.

But the overriding reason for the Bible's hold on me is the access it can give to God. He surely is the reason for treating the Bible reverently, even those passages which are difficult to accept as they stand. The Bible can communicate timeless and eternal truths, uplifting our spirits, challenging our minds and enriching our faith. It is the most profound and significant vehicle for the word of God.

Approaching the Bible today can seem a little daunting; in many ways it is a very difficult book to understand. The very size of the Bible can seem formidable — sixty-six books in all, each containing a variety of different types of material — let alone the fact that it reflects cultures and societies bewilderingly different from our own. It is not surprising that many modern people wonder about its relevance in today's world. The Bible needs an interpreter to help translate it into a meaningful form. I am writing this book for the Bible Reading Fellowship whose ministry is dedicated to precisely this — helping people to hear the Bible addressing itself to them now.

In this book, I invite you to look at well-known scriptural passages with me, exploring them as visual and literary images, and interpreting them in the light of our common experience. The Bible can be seen as a huge art gallery, full of colourful and vivid masterpieces, and it is this idea which I have used here. We can imagine ourselves moving from one picture to another, pointing out details, sharing our responses and reflecting on the meaning of what the artist is trying to say through the painting they have created. There are many other biblical masterpieces besides the thirty I have selected — perhaps I could say they represent my own private collection of personal favourites. But I hope that by sharing this approach to the Bible with you it will help you to see and experience its immense richness and variety. And when we do experience the Bible, hearing some word of God addressed to us by the Holy Spirit who is the divine interpreter, the only appropriate response is to pray. This is why I have added prayers to the readings which follow.

THE OLD TESTAMENT

No easy answer

3 Now the serpent was more subtil than any beast of the field which the Lord God had made. And he said unto the woman, 'Yea, hath God said, "Ye shall not eat of every tree of the garden"?' ²And the woman said unto the serpent, 'We may eat of the fruit of the trees of the garden: ³But of the fruit of the tree which is in the midst of the garden, God hath said, "Ye shall not eat of it, neither shall ye touch it, lest ye die"'. ⁴And the serpent said unto the woman, 'Ye shall not surely die: ⁵for God doth know that in the day ye eat thereof, then your eyes shall be opened, and ye shall be as gods, knowing good and evil'. ⁶And when the woman saw that the tree was good for food, and that it was pleasant to the eyes, and a tree to be desired to make one wise, she took of the fruit thereof, and did eat, and gave also unto her husband with her; and he did eat.

Genesis 3.1—6 (AV)

You are looking at a garden, a superb place. Everything you could wish for is here — luscious food, stupendous beauty, peace and tranquility. How could such a rich environment fail to produce happiness? Or, let me look at the picture from another angle. Provide a community with a splendid environment, with money and yet more money, with every facility and gadget, and, most importantly, with freedom for everyone to do just what they want to do. The result will be . . . what, I wonder? That is the question. And the answer the picture gives us is this: the outcome will be profoundly disappointing. And we don't believe it; we don't want to believe it. We turn away hurriedly on to the next exhibit — we may even leave the art gallery altogether, not a little disgusted.

But somehow we can't erase the picture from our minds. Michelangelo felt compelled to paint it on the ceiling of the Sistine Chapel in the Vatican at Rome. That woman, that serpent, that forbidden fruit. We drag ourselves back for another look. The author of this narrative in Genesis must have been only too aware that what is forbidden is immediately attractive — watch any schoolboy. But what he is also saying is that some things in any garden, however attractive, are by their nature poisonous to humans and are best avoided. So are some practices in life.

We, however, are tempted by them. It is some comfort to know that in the first place, the temptation derives from something outside ourselves, not from an *essential* badness within us all. But the poisonous berries in the garden look so good. No one could know that they were poisonous merely by looking at them. So the temptation to try them is craftily formulated. In the Genesis picture, it is represented by a snake, a sly, wriggling, deceitful creature. It does not come roaring at its adversary like a tiger bearing its teeth. You are not aware of it until it is there. What is more, it is beautifully marked. Some people are fascinated by snakes.

So the temptation to experiment with practices we know to be harmful is most likely to be planted in our consciousness in the first place subtly by some casual remark in a general conversation. 'Well, everybody does it, don't they?', or, rather more subtly, 'Would a good God have provided this attraction if not for our benefit?'

But the woman was not immediately caught. She retorted with the reminder of God's prohibition, even strengthening it. God had not actually said the tree was not to be *touched*. This was the woman's addition, but it showed how the prohibition rankled. The tempter at once saw his chance and met that slight weakness in her with a bold attack in the form of a strong assertion: 'ye shall not surely die: For God doth know that in the day ye eat thereof, then your eyes shall be opened, and ye shall be as gods, knowing good and evil'.

This is the way to win — every politician knows it; tell people what you want them to believe without 'batting an eyelid' and the odds are they will believe you, especially if you repeat it again and again. But if you argue with them they will only argue back. First make assertions and then, if need be, bring in your supporting arguments. The tempter had yet another trick and quickly played it. 'You are being hoodwinked by the prohibition. God does not want a man to rival his achievement! What is more, rules produce inner conflicts through repression. Break them then and grow up!'

So when the woman looked again at the tree of knowledge with its brilliant berries she was gripped by its triple appeal. It is 'good

for food', that is profitable: it is 'pleasant to the eyes', so aestheti-
cally and sensually attractive: and it is 'to make one wise', an even
more alluring promise of lasting power to add to the immediate
satisfaction. So she fell for the temptation and ate the fruit, giving it
also to her husband and he ate. And we may suppose the snake
wriggled away giggling at his easy win, if snakes do giggle. It had
achieved its purpose.

*　　*　　*

The perfect environment is not, after all, the answer to human happiness, because in every environment there have to be restrictions
as well as liberties. Everyone is not able to do as he or she likes. That
is the bit we resent. And that is where the breakdown occurs, or —
to employ the traditional, theological word — the fall. We insist on
having *unlimited* freedom and that is fatal. If we can bear to look at
this uncomfortable scene a little longer, we realize that it depicts a
process which is happening every day in our own lives; temptation
is an integral part of our humanity. And we cannot change our
nature 'to be like gods', but have to accept our place within a limited
framework. If we do so, we can use our freedom to create happiness
rather than destroy it.

Prayer

> O God, who knowest us to be set in the midst of so
> many and great dangers, that by reason of the frailty
> of our nature we cannot always stand upright: grant
> to us such strength and protection, as we may support
> us in all dangers, and carry us through all
> temptations; through Jesus Christ our Lord.
>
> *From the Book of Common Prayer*

Called to serve

³¹Terah took Abram his son and Lot the son of Haran, his grandson, and Sarai his daughter-in-law, his son Abram's wife, and they went forth together from Ur of the Chaldeans to go into the land of Canaan; but when they came to Haran, they settled there. ³²The days of Terah were two hundred and five years; and Terah died in Haran.
12 Now the Lord said to Abram, 'Go from your country and your kindred and your father's house to the land that I will show you. ²And I will make of you a great nation, and I will bless you, and make your name great, so that you will be a blessing'.

Genesis 11.31—12.2 (RSV)

This is a small picture but a significant one, for it fixes for all time an epoch-making event. Abram (later called Abraham) sets off to leave Ur of the Chaldees, a city in Southern Babylonia. He breaks with land, kindred, and family connections — no mean severance when we consider that to ancient people, living in closely knit cultures, breaking ancestral bonds in this way was almost unthinkable. But the responsibility for the future of Israel lies on the shoulders of this one man. God intervenes in history and grants his divine promise or blessing to Abram and his descendants. Abram is called, or 'elected', to be the recipient and mediator of this divine blessing; he is invited to abandon his security and pursue an unknown destiny.

Many people find the idea of 'election' offensive in some way: it is as if God has a special list of favourites who are chosen for no merit of their own. Indeed, no reason is given as to why Abram is chosen to lead Israel into a new land and a new era. Surely, this is élitism plain and simple, fixed in the Bible before we have scarcely begun to turn its pages? What is more, this picture introduces the dominant biblical theme of a 'chosen people' — another objectionable idea to some. But we have to come to look again at this picture if we are to grasp its deeper meaning.

Notice that the Bible mentions nothing of the pain and preparations, the doubts and possibly resentment that must have plagued Abram. Unlike some of the Genesis stories, which reveal the patriarchs wrestling with their faith and often giving in to all too human temptations, there is no indication of Abram's feelings here. Instead, the focus of attention is very much on God himself, and his action in history. God calls, guides, sustains, and reassures humanity. The main purpose of this biblical picture, then, is not so much to introduce us to the idea of election or a chosen people as to highlight the guiding and protective hand of God in the affairs of all men and women.

Abram is the father of all those down the ages who have been called to service in a special way. We all have our special talents and may even have a sense of vocation, but some have been chosen to serve God and their community in a more direct way. It is always God's strategy to mediate his blessing to all humanity through individuals, often the most unlikely people — not spotless, or fault-less, and certainly not all saintly. Looking at our picture of Abram, we soon begin to realize that people are not chosen for their own comfort; they must often be prepared for a life of self-sacrifice, even suffering, on behalf of others. Their calling is not for privilege but for service — and a very costly one at that. We only have to think of someone like Mother Teresa, or Mahatma Ghandi for instance, to see God at work through individuals and the kind of sacrifices they are called to make.

★   ★   ★

The story of Abram's call shows us that, as Christians, we, too, must be prepared to give up our own familiar surroundings and routines in order to set off in a completely different direction. If we are receptive and obedient to our own calling we will open up a vital relationship in which God can work in and through our lives. We will need a lot of strength and trust, but God will bless us and remind us of his plans for us; it is our attitude and response to those plans which determine our relationship with God.

Prayer

> Lord, every day you call us out into the unknown,
> every day we journey one day further on.
> Every day there are traps and pitfalls,
> not least of doubt and fearfulness.

What does the future hold for me
and all I hold most dear?
Lord, give me grace to trust your loving kindness.

Wrestling with life

[9]And Jacob said, 'O God of my father Abraham and God of my father Isaac, O Lord who didst say to me, "Return to your country and to your kindred, and I will do you good", [10]I am not worthy of the least of all the steadfast love and all the faithfulness which thou hast shown to thy servant, for with only my staff I crossed this Jordan; and now I have become two companies. [11]Deliver me, I pray thee, from the hand of my brother, from the hand of Esau, for I fear him' . . .

[13]So he lodged there that night, and took from what he had with him a present for his brother Esau . . . [20]For he thought, 'I may appease him with the present that goes before me, and afterwards I shall see his face; perhaps he will accept me' . . . [22]The same night he arose and took his two wives, his two maids, and his eleven children, and crossed the ford of the Jabbok. [23]He took them and sent them across the stream, and likewise everything that he had. [24]And Jacob was left alone; and a man wrestled with him until the breaking of the day. [25]When the man saw that he did not prevail against Jacob, he touched the hollow of his thigh; and Jacob's thigh was put out of joint as he wrestled with him. [26]Then he said, 'Let me go, for the day is breaking'. But Jacob said, 'I will not let you go, unless you bless me'. [27]And he said to him, 'What is your name?' And he said, 'Jacob'. [28]Then he said, 'Your name shall no more be called Jacob, but Israel, for you have striven with God and with men, and have prevailed'. [29]Then Jacob asked him, 'Tell me, I pray, your name'. But he said, 'Why is it that you ask my name?' And there he blessed him. [30]So Jacob called the name of the place Peniel, saying, 'For I have seen God face to face, and yet my life is preserved'.

Genesis 32, selected verses (RSV)

This scene has puzzled a great many readers. It is the wrestling which catches our attention: Jacob wrestling with a mysterious figure and no clear victor emerging. What are we to make of this picture? Was there really a physical confrontation at all? Or are we looking at a pictorial representation of a struggle in the mind, indeed in the soul, of Jacob?

Over and over again, all night long, alone in the dark, Jacob reviewed the strange way life — or God — had led him. And to-morrow he would face a crisis. Nothing concentrates the mind so much as an impending crisis, transforming the night into a lonely battlefield. For Jacob, that night had been the turning point of his life. He became a different man with a different name — Israel instead of Jacob. He reckoned he had come 'face to face' with God.

We shall never really make sense of this picture unless we go back in Jacob's story seeing it in a broader perspective. The key lies in that incident years before when Jacob tricked his brother Esau out of his birthright and had to flee the country (Genesis 27.1—28.10). Jacob had crossed the River Jordan all those years ago with nothing but his staff, but now his riches consisted of cattle and servants: he had amassed great wealth and a large family. To-morrow he would have to face once more his brother whom he had cheated. Could Esau be appeased with a present — a large present? Call it a bribe if you must. Would all that he had gained be taken away from him?

With such troubling prospects and thoughts, Jacob watched his possessions cross the ford of the Jabbock, and he was left alone — alone with his past, alone to face the fearful future. He was still there when darkness fell, still wrestling with his thoughts, and he could not sleep. Very little had his possessions given him in the way of peace of mind. They had crowded it out and cramped his soul. As the dawn was breaking, he was broken of his over-weening self-sufficiency, broken of his independence of any need of help from anyone, including God. But in the broken-ness of that experience God once again became the reality to him he had been in his youth.

Jacob did not lose his fear of Esau overnight. He did not back down on his decision to try and soften his brother with a present. But when he did meet Esau, the encounter was not in the least what he had expected. So Jacob was not after all the lonely man he thought he was; God was going before him to prepare the way. After that terrible night of wrestling he knew now.

★   ★   ★

13

There are times in our lives when we find ourselves struggling with our innermost conflicts, coming 'face to face' with our own stark reality. Our whole being is tossed and turned in every direction. Our past becomes an abyss of emotions we would rather not face, our future, a stretch of unnavigated waters full of crises and daunting situations. We are caught in the midst of it all, wrestling with the experience of life. Like Jacob, we need to put aside our possessions and 'props' occasionally to face what is beyond. If we do not turn our backs on God, for all our failings, God will not turn his back on us. It is a lesson most of us do not learn until in some way we have been broken.

Prayer

> Lead us, heavenly Father, lead us
> O'er the the world's tempestuous sea;
> Guard us, guide us, keep us, feed us,
> For we have no help but thee;
> Yet possessing every blessing,
> If our God our Father be.

From Hymns Ancient and Modern

Saved to save

2 Now a man from the house of Levi went and took to wife a daughter of Levi. [2]The woman conceived and bore a son; and when she saw that he was a goodly child, she hid him three months. [3]And when she could hide him no longer she took for him a basket made of bulrushes, and daubed it with bitumen and pitch; and she put the child in it and placed it among the reeds at the river's brink. [4]And his sister stood at a distance, to know what would be done to him. [5]Now the daughter of Pharaoh came down to bathe at the river, and her maidens walked beside the river; she saw the basket among the reeds and sent her maid to fetch it. [6]When she opened it she saw the child; and lo, the babe was crying. She took pity on him and said, 'This is one of the Hebrews' children'. [7]Then his sister said to Pharaoh's daughter, 'Shall I go and call you a nurse from the Hebrew women to nurse the child for you?' [8]And Pharaoh's daughter said to her, 'Go'. So the girl went and called the child's mother. [9]And Pharaoh's daughter said to her, 'Take this child away, and nurse him for me, and I will give you your wages'. So the woman took the child and nursed him. [10]And the child grew, and she brought him to Pharaoh's daughter, and he became her son; and she named him Moses, for she said, 'Because I drew him out of the water'.

Exodus 2.1−10 (RSV)

Here we encounter attempted genocide, that is the extermination of a whole class or race. The Pharaoh of Egypt in 1290-1224 BC, Rameses II, adopted this abhorrent policy towards the Hebrew settlers in his territory in case, increasing in number and power, they became a threat to the stability of the State in time of war. He ordered all male babies born to the Hebrews to be tossed into the Nile. Such is the background of this picture. We do have twentieth-century examples of merciless tyrants attempting to wipe out nations, which makes this image all the more potent.

It is impossible to imagine the intense grief in Egypt among the Hebrew families. Picture the trek to the river with a babe-in-arms about to drown it. Every mother must have dreaded having children in case she gave birth to a boy, only to be torn away from her in the most brutal way possible. This nightmare of suffering, then, forms the framework of our picture here where the focus is on one particular mother. Having given birth to a beautifully formed, a perfect baby boy, she could not bring herself to trek down to the river. She procrastinated, hiding her baby until it was no longer possible to hide him. Then she had an idea — an outrageous idea. Yes, she would take her baby to the river and come back without him, but she would not drown him in the Nile, she would leave him floating on the water. She devised a plan. Taking an ordinary basket made of bulrushes, she waterproofed it with bitumen and pitch: even with the weight of the baby it would float. She placed her baby inside, covered it with the lid of the basket, lodged it carefully half-hidden among the shorter reeds at the river's brink where the tide would not sweep it out into the main stream, and waited. The

15

place had been carefully selected. It was the point on the river bank where Pharaoh's daughter was accustomed to bathe. She might see the basket. She might be intrigued to know what it was. She might lift the lid. Then she would see the baby. And she might be touched, deeply touched. She was a woman, even though she was the daughter of the very Pharaoh who had instigated the policy of genocide. The chance of the baby's survival was one in a thousand against, but the plan was her only hope.

And would the princess come down to the water that day? She did come down, into the water, her servants on the bank shielding her privacy as was customary. There was, however, a girl not far away watching — the baby's older sister, sent by her mother to see what became of the baby in the basket. What she saw was the princess in the shallow water, her attention caught by a strange object lodged in the reeds. The princess called a servant to recover it, who opening it discovered the baby, a little boy crying. The princess' heart was touched. Hebrew or no Hebrew she was captivated by the baby's appealing helplessness. The girl on the bank, with feminine intuition, young as she was, read the signs: the princess longed to possess that child. Coming forward, the young girl made an offer: 'Shall I call a Hebrew woman to nurse the child for you?' The offer was accepted, and the girl brought not a woman, but the baby's own mother. The princess offered the mother wages to be the child's nurse, in doing so claiming him for herself. So this male Hebrew baby was saved from drowning and grew up in an Egyptian palace as the princess' adopted son.

★   ★   ★

If this picture of what happened one day on the banks of the Nile does nothing else but remind us of the essential ministry of women and its motivation, it will not have been painted in vain. But there is more. Look over the verses and see how not a single name is provided except that of Moses. The spotlight is turned and left on him. It was Moses who was saved, and he it was who came to lead the Hebrews away from the threat of genocide in Egypt. Moses was therefore saved in order to save his people. Notice how, in this picture, there is no mention of God, no intimation of anything miraculous, nothing explicitly theological, only womanly love and womanly ingenuity. But God was at work. Just as Moses was to be God's agent carrying out his purposes for Israel and for mankind so, too, the women were agents and had an equally vital role to play in the overall scheme of things. And where God is at work, although the plan may appear to hang on the slenderest of threads, the Bible assures us that there is ultimately not the slightest risk of failure; it is as safe as if it were suspended on a hawser made of steel. Moses was safe in his little basket on the mighty waters of the River Nile as was Jesus in his improvized cradle in the stable at Bethlehem, even though Herod raged without, because God wanted him; he was saved to save.

Prayer

> Lord, I thank you that I have not drowned
>> in the waters of affliction, of doubt, of sinfulness,
>>> and of self-centredness or constant anxiety.
>> I have come close to drowning.
> But you have saved me
>> through the love of people holding me up,
>> mother, wife, sister, friend;
>> through simple actions and attitudes
>> rather more than by what was said;
>> through the fellowship of the church to which I belong.
> Lord, I do not know from what you have saved me
>> but that you are the Saviour, I am sure,
>> and I shall not drown so long as I hold to you.
> Thanks be to you, O Lord, my strong deliverer.

The battle is the Lord's

---

6 Now Jericho was shut up from within and from without because of the people of Israel; none went out, and none came in. ²And the Lord said to Joshua, 'See, I have given into your hand Jericho, with its king and mighty men of valour. ³You shall march around the city, all the men of war going around the city once. Thus shall you do for six days. [4]And seven priests shall bear seven trumpets of rams' horns before the ark; and on the seventh day you shall march around the city seven times, the priests blowing the trumpets. [5]And when they make a long blast with the ram's horn, as soon as you hear the sound of the trumpet, then all the people shall shout with a great shout; and the wall of the city will fall down flat, and the people shall go up every man straight before him".

Joshua 6.1—5 (RSV)

We can see Jericho well enough in this picture; shut city gates, walls manned day and night; swords, spears, daggers and axes sharpened and ready, probably barrels of boiling pitch all at hand to repel the invaders. But what we cannot see is the crippling anxiety in the hearts of the people locked in the city over the terrifying uncertainty about the next day. There was absolutely nothing that could be done but to wait — and the waiting was cruel.

And below Jericho's walls on the banks of the River Jordan the armies of Israel waited, toughened by their stay in the desert, convinced that God had promised them this land and Jericho, the gateway to it. They, too, were waiting — waiting for a signal from Joshua, their Commander-in-Chief, to begin the assault. But no call to arms came. Instead a call to a religious drama, a kind of act of worship complete with robed priests, ceremonial trumpets, and, central to everything, the sacred box or ark of the covenant being carried, signifying the real presence of God.

Notice the battle instructions to the Israelite army, 'You shall march around the city, all the men of war going around the city once. Thus shall you do for six days. And seven priests shall bear seven trumpets of rams' horns before the ark; and on the seventh day you shall march around the city seven times, the priests blowing the trumpets'. Does this not strike us as utterly ridiculous? An army is unable to destroy a fortress by walking around it once, let alone seven times! Nevertheless, for a whole week this apparent farce continued, and, of course, not a single gate was opened, not a single rampart toppled. Yet there was the ark of the covenant, the symbol of God's real presence, in their midst; he had promised to give them the city and the land it guarded. That promise must have taken some believing in front of Jericho's massive walls. If ever there was a test of faith in God's word, this was it. And what of the inhabitants of Jericho manning the walls and staring at this astonishing spectacle day after day? What was the strategy? What was the trick? Were the Israelites fooling them? If the faith of the encircling Israelites was being sorely tested, the resolution of the defending people of Jericho was yet more. They were, in fact, being slowly worn down.

Then the seventh day dawned and with it the trek around the city seven times. Now surely Joshua would give the signal for the attack. Every soldier, we may be sure, put a firm grip on his weapon. This was it! There came the expected long blast on the ram's horn, and the whole army as instructed raised its voice in a tremendous shout surely believing this to be the battle cry initiating the assault. Now they would fight their way into the city and take it. But nothing like this happened: there was no need. Instead, the walls of the fortified city simply collapsed and the army walked in. They had not taken the city by the force of their arms at all; the Lord had *given them* the city as he had promised.

★　★　★

More than likely we stand increduously smiling before this picture in the biblical art gallery. Life's battles are not won in this fashion — we wish they were. Or maybe if we stop to consider the story at all seriously, we might be interested to know what really happened historically to inspire this extraordinary scene, and we might turn up some reports of archeological investigations of the site to provide perhaps evidence of Jericho's walls being collapsed by an earthquake and falling outwards, facilitating the military assault. We are not trying to explain rationally the content of our pictures, though. We are concerned with the impact and power of these biblical masterpieces and how they reflect truths in our own lives. Here surely, in this strange assault story, we are being asked to come to terms with the religious insight that sometimes, perhaps more often than we, with our twentieth-century incredulity, are willing to recognize, God does give astonishing victories in the battles of life to those who look to him for guidance, and trust in the promise of his care. The battleground could be a severe sickness, mental or physical, a tangle of family or business problems seemingly impossible to unravel, poverty, unemployment or a crippling fear of the future. This biblical masterpiece of Jericho's overthrow warns us not to cast out the possibility that God will fight our battle

19

for us if we have faith in him. Of course our faith will be tested. It was tested at Jericho. And sometimes waiting for God to act will appear farcical. But an active willingness to be taken wherever God might lead us will help us today face our own tomorrow.

Prayer

Lord, I confess
　　how easily, and how often, I fall
　　　into the trap of thinking
　　that everything in my life and about my life
　　depends on me, my own efforts, and my own skills.
　　I hear of your promise of strength,
　　your grace to help in time of need
　　and the victory that overcomes even our faith,
　　but I act as if the battle of my life
　　is mine and not yours.
Lord, I will believe in you today,
　　believe that you care for me
　　and that you hold me in your hands.
Lord, I believe; help my unbelief.

Spiritual roots

[21]And the Philistines seized him and gouged out his eyes, and brought him down to Gaza, and bound him with bronze fetters; and he ground at the mill in the prison. [22]But the hair of his head began to grow again after it had been shaved.

[23]Now the lords of the Philistines gathered to offer a great sacrifice to Dagon their god, and to rejoice; for they said, 'Our god has given Samson our enemy into our hand'. [24]And when the people saw him, they praised their god; for they said, 'Our god has given our enemy into our hand, the ravager of our country, who has slain many of us'. [25]And when their hearts were merry, they said, 'Call Samson, that he

may make sport for us'. So they called Samson out of the prison, and he made sport before them. They made him stand between the pillars; ²⁶and Samson said to the lad who held him by the hand, 'Let me feel the pillars on which the house rests, that I may lean against them'. ²⁷Now the house was full of men and women; all the lords of the Philistines were there, and on the roof there were about three thousand men and women, who looked on while Samson made sport.

²⁸Then Samson called to the Lord and said, 'O Lord God, remember me, I pray thee, and strengthen me, I pray thee, only this once, O God, that I may be avenged upon the Philistines for one of my two eyes'. ²⁹And Samson grasped the two middle pillars upon which the house rested, and he leaned his weight upon them, his right hand on the one and his left hand on the other. ³⁰And Samson said, 'Let me die with the Philistines'. Then he bowed with all his might; and the house fell upon the lords and upon all the people that were in it. So the dead whom he slew at his death were more than those whom he had slain during his life. ³¹Then his brothers and all his family came down and took him and brought him up and buried him between Zorah and Eshtaol in the tomb of Manoah his father . . .

Judges 16.21—31 (RSV)

'There are some rum things in the Bible', the late King George V is reported to have said after struggling to read it. And of course, there are some very 'rum' things, if the Bible is taken to be a record of the lives of saints. Not by any stretch of the imagination, for instance, could Samson be classed as a saint. He possessed no moral elevation whatsoever and nothing in the way of religious aims, let alone achievements. Samson's character suggests something of a ruffian who victimized his enemies, the Philistines, to their intense frustration and hurt. They were enemies to him because they constantly harried his people, Israel, but this did not deter him from taking an attractive Philistine woman to be his wife. It seems Samson lacked principles. Moreover, he organized no military campaign against the Philistines, lacking the leadership qualities required. His only tactic was a sort of taunting one-man guerilla warfare based on his stupendous physical strength. It is hard to find anything in Samson to admire.

No estimate of Samson is complete without taking into account his long, uncut hair. Fashion did not dictate it, nor was laziness the clue, but rather a religious vow, not made by him but by his parents before birth. He was made a Nazirite which meant notably that no

21

razor must touch his head and no wine pass his lips. Samson kept that vow. It was about the only rule he did keep. He never cut his hair. And so this ebullient ruffian went joyfully terrorizing the Philistine/Israel border, maintaining through all his crude and coarse activities this one secret — an unbroken, flimsy, root connection with God. Somewhere deep down inside him was this point of relationship with spiritual reality, which was the secret source of his strength. No one knew; perhaps he scarcely knew it himself. He did not intend that anyone should know. Let people puzzle, let even the wife of his bosom puzzle wherein his great strength lay, for he was no *obvious* giant. So Samson stands as the father of all those down the ages whom no one would guess have any spiritual spring of action whatsoever, but it is there, hidden, and apparently not quite dead but dormant. And then in some unexpected desperate situation it is faintly perceived. This is what the picture of Samson in Gaza gives us in the story here.

In the picture we have before us, Samson is free to terrorize no more. Instead we see him a prisoner in a Gaza gaol, caught by the Philistines, his Philistine wife having cut his hair and wheedled out of him the secret source of his strength. With his hair cut, his eyes gouged out, his limbs bound with fatters of brass he looks a sorrowful sight as he grinds corn in the prison house, humiliated. Then one day at some wild party in Gaza he is brought out on to a public stage to be prodded into acts of buffoonery for the amusement of a mammoth drunken audience. This is the last straw: he can bear his degradation no longer.

Samson called to the boy who attended him in his blindness to let him feel the pillars on which the great building was supported. He knew his hair had begun to grow again and dimly he knew the spiritual source of strength it signified. So he prayed. Granted, not much of a prayer. There was little of spirituality in it, but he prayed nevertheless. It is the only occasion of which we are told that he prayed. 'O Lord God, remember me, I pray thee, and strengthen me, I pray thee, only this once, O God, that I may be at once avenged for my two eyes.' Then taking hold of the pillars he said, 'Let me die with the Philistines'. And bowing himself with all his might he sent the whole building crashing down, crushing to death the crowds packed in to mock. 'So', the narrator of this story wrote ironically, 'the dead whom he slew at his death were more than those whom he had slain during his life'.

★   ★   ★

Is there nothing more to escape our lips than a sigh as we view this macabre heap of mangled corpses and Samson's body sufficiently recognizable to be gathered up for reverent burial beside his father? But suppose Samson has been brought to our attention as a kind of impersonation of Israel. Suppose the story is proclaiming the truth that the nation could only be strong so long as it maintained its dedication to God. Suppose it is declaring that it will be enfeebled if it allows itself to be infatuated by the incongruity of sensual desires, and pagan gods. Is there not a message here, and one not only for ancient Israel but for our own contemporary situation? In the modern world, when materialism, hedonism and general licence take over, a nation is vulnerable. Lasting strength, strength for constructive and not destructive aims, needs spiritual roots. Most nations only learn this lesson the hard way. The story of Samson may be a crude one in many ways, but it has this salutary lesson to impart. We would be wise to take it to heart.

Prayer

Lord of all power and might, who art the author and giver of all good things: graft in our hearts the love of thy name, increase in us true religion, nourish us with all goodness, and of thy great mercy keep us in the same; through Jesus Christ our Lord.

From the Book of Common Prayer

God's grace, our foolishness

1 There was a certain man of Ramathaim-zophim of the hill country of Ephraim, whose name was Elkanah the son of Jeroham, son of Elihu, son of Tohu, son of Zuph, an Ephraimite. ²He had two wives; the name of the one was Hannah, and the name of the other Peninnah. And Peninnah had children, but Hannah had no children.

[3]Now this man used to go up year by year from his city to worship and to sacrifice to the Lord of hosts at Shiloh, where the two sons of Eli, Hophni and Phinehas, were priests of the Lord. [4]On the day when Elkanah sacrificed, he would give portions to Peninnah his wife and to all her sons and daughters; [5]and, although he loved Hannah, he would give Hannah only one portion, because the Lord had closed her womb. [6]And her rival used to provoke her sorely, to irritate her, because the Lord had closed her womb. [7]So it went on year by year; as often as she went up to the house of the Lord, she used to provoke her. Therefore Hannah wept and would not eat. [8]And Elkanah, her husband, said to her, 'Hannah, why do you weep? And why do you not eat? And why is your heart sad? Am I not more to you than ten sons?'

[9]After they had eaten and drunk in Shiloh, Hannah rose. Now Eli the priest was sitting on the seat beside the doorpost of the temple of the Lord. [10]She was deeply distressed and prayed to the Lord, and wept bitterly. [11]And she vowed a vow and said, 'O Lord of hosts, if thou wilt indeed look on the affliction of thy maidservant, and remember me, and not forget thy maidservant, but wilt give to thy maidservant a son, then I will give him to the Lord all the days of his life, and no razor shall touch his head'.

[12]As she continued praying before the Lord, Eli observed her mouth. [13]Hannah was speaking in her heart; only her lips moved, and her voice was not heard; therefore Eli took her to be a drunken woman. [14]And Eli said to her, 'How long will you be drunken? Put away your wine from you'. [15]But Hannah answered, 'No, my lord, I am a woman sorely troubled; I have drunk neither wine nor strong drink, but I have been pouring out my soul before the Lord. [16]Do not regard your maidservant as a base woman, for all along I have been speaking out of my great anxiety and vexation'. [17]Then Eli answered, 'Go in peace, and the God of Israel grant your petition which you have made to him'. [18]And she said, 'Let your maidservant find favour in your eyes'. Then the woman went her way and ate, and her countenance was no longer sad.

[19]They rose early in the morning and worshipped before the Lord; then they went back to their house at Ramah. And Elkanah knew Hannah his wife, and the Lord remembered her; [20]and in due time Hannah conceived and bore a son, and she called his name Samuel, for she said, 'I have asked him of the Lord'.

1 Samuel 1.1—20 (RSV)

Why did you do it, Elkanah? You were a good man, a kindly man, a man most diligent over your religious observances. Assiduously once a year you left your house in Ramah to attend the appointed festival at the temple in Shiloh; and your pedigree was a model; you were an honourable man. But, were you lacking in worldly wisdom? Religious people can sometimes be extraordinarily dim-witted! Were you one of those simple souls, sheltered from your youth who occasionally makes the most stupid blunders? Surely you must have known that if you take two women at the same time into your life, whatever the custom or fashion, there will be trouble?

What happened? We do not know exactly but it looks as if Elkanah fell madly in love with Hannah. But for all the love he gave her she bore him no children, and that in the culture of the time was a disgrace. A woman might as well not be born as to be barren. And she cried her heart out, as well she might. But what is marriage for but to produce a family? This was the sore question Elkanah asked himself. He had come from a good family: his family tree was carefully preserved. So he took another woman, Peninnah, *in order to have a family.* Two women in the same house at Ramah! No, Elkanah did not love Peninnah as he loved Hannah. But she bore children, both sons and daughters. By her Elkanah became a father and founded a family who might one day bring him credit and fame.

As each child was born to Peninnah so Hannah fretted the more. It was all very well that Elkanah should spell out his love for her — 'Am I not more to you than ten sons?' But he had no idea of how one woman will 'take it out of another' whom she knows is more highly esteemed by the shared man. Peninnah with her sharp tongue made Hannah's life a misery. Year after year it went on, and insult was piled on injury by Elkanah, that religious but dim-witted man; at each annual festival at Shiloh, when each pilgrim offered a sacrifice, he saw to it that to Peninnah was allotted portions for all the members of her family but to Hannah one portion only for herself, worthy enough but advertising her loneliness. What short-sighted stupidity!

And now we see poor faded Hannah coming before that old and decrepit priest, praying for a baby boy whom she would dedicate to God. And Eli so far gone in natural as well as spiritual perception that he supposed her drunk because her lips moved but no voice was heard. Poor Hannah! He even rebuked her. Shame on the man! She was driven to defend herself and declare her heart broken. But that Eli was not hopelessly worthless as a priest was shown by the blessing he gave her — 'Go in peace, and the God of Israel grant your petition which you have made to him.' And Hannah believed;

in fact, she so trusted that she was no more sad. No wonder that
Elkanah seeing the revival of her spirit and her beauty loved her
passionately, and she conceived and bore a son. Samuel, her
longed-for baby boy, grew to be the first in the great line of prophets in Israel and the founder of the monarchy. There is hardly in
Hebrew history a name greater than Samuel; his fame and influence were immense.

★ ★ ★

The overwhelmingly human qualities of the characters painted in
the scene endear us towards them. Perhaps we can see ourselves
reflected back at us in the resentment of Peninnah, the anguish of
Hannah, the weakness of Eli, but most of all in the foolishness of
Elkanah. But it is here where the gospel, the message of good news,
can be found in this picture. We may be foolish, we may commit
acts of stupidity, and gross short-sightedness, often simply following the current fashion, but if our heart is right before God as was
Elkanah's and as was Hannah's, God's grace will overtop our
shortcomings and blessing will arise from the very ground of our
foolishness.

Prayer

> Lord, I haven't always been wise.
>> Sometimes, indeed, I have been very foolish.
>> But I meant well, I really did.
>> Forgive me, Lord,
>> And help something good to come out of my stupidity.
>> You are my gracious and merciful Lord.

Five smooth stones

---

17 Now the Philistines gathered their armies for battle; . . . ²And Saul
and the men of Israel were gathered, and encamped in the valley of

Elah, and drew up in line of battle against the Philistines. [3]And the Philistines stood on the mountain on the one side, and Israel stood on the mountain on the other side, with a valley between them. [4]And there came out from the camp of the Philistines a champion named Goliath, of Gath, whose height was six cubits and a span . . . [8]He stood and shouted to the ranks of Israel, 'Why have you come out to draw up for battle? Am I not a Philistine, and are you not servants of Saul? Choose a man for yourselves, and let him come down to me. [9]If he is able to fight with me and kill me, then we will be your servants; but if I prevail against him and kill him, then you shall be our servants and serve us' . . .

[32]And David said to Saul, 'Let no man's heart fail because of him; your servant will go and fight with this Philistine'. [33]And Saul said to David, 'You are not able to go against this Philistine to fight with him; for you are but a youth, and he has been a man of war from his youth'. [34]But David said to Saul, . . . [36]'Your servant has killed both lions and bears; . . . [37]The Lord who delivered me from the paw of the lion and from the paw of the bear, will deliver me from the hand of this Philistine'. And Saul said to David, 'Go, and the Lord be with you!' [38]Then Saul clothed David with his armour; . . . [39]Then David said to Saul, 'I cannot go with these; for I am not used to them' . . . [40]Then he took his staff in his hand, and chose five smooth stones from the brook, and put them in his shepherd's bag or wallet; his sling was in his hand, and he drew near to the Philistine . . .

[48]When the Philistine arose and came and drew near to meet David, David ran quickly toward the battle line to meet the Philistine. [49]And David put his hand in his bag and took out a stone, and slung it, and struck the Philistine on his forehead; the stone sank into his forehead, and he fell on his face to the ground.

[50]So David prevailed over the Philistine with a sling and with a stone, and struck the Philistine, and killed him; there was no sword in the hand of David.

1 Samuel 17, selected verses (RSV)

In this picture, we see two armies trapped by the situation in which they were drawn up, the Philistines and the Israelites, deadly enemies, each out to crush the other, but the nature of the terrain at Shochoh constituted a military impasse. Neither dared approach the other in that narrow valley exposing themselves to the enemy artillery as they descended to the brook at the bottom and slowing down to cross it. Goaded, therefore, by the futility of merely bawling insults at each other, the Philistines proposed that the question of superiority be decided by a warrior from each side engaging in single combat. The Philistines felt safe with this proposal since they boasted a giant of a man, Goliath, eight feet tall with the strength and bulk of a bull. He was covered in protective brazen armour and carried as weapons a sword and a spear. Israel had no one to compare with him.

Then David, a shepherd boy, appeared on the scene carrying food from his father Jesse at home to his brothers serving in the Israelite army. David saw the armies locked in the valley and heard Goliath of Gath roaring out his abuses of Israel. He noted his giant size and estimated his formidable strength, but he was not afraid of him. When this was reported to Saul, the royal commander of the Israelite army, he sent for him. And when David declared his willingness to go to 'fight with this Philistine', not surprisingly Saul voiced the absurdity of a mere youth in mortal combat with this bawling, bulky bear from Gath, trained for war. But David continued to protest his prowess in dangerous situations and eventually Saul agreed to let him go. After all, there would be no insult to the Israelite army and no further weakening of morale if Goliath killed a mere shepherd boy and not a seasoned soldier. So he rigged out David in his armour and with his weapons. David must have been thrilled with this royal accoutrement, but he divested himself of it all. He could not fight with untried weapons.

And then, absolutely alone with nothing but his staff, his shepherd's bag on his shoulder and his sling, he crossed that ravine. No onlooker could believe his eyes. There must have been an awesome silence from both sides. Goliath roared his insults, attempting to ridicule the fragile-looking youth being sent to do battle with him. But, quite unshaken, David cried back, 'You come to me with a sword and with a spear and with a javelin; but I come to you in the name of the Lord of hosts, the God of the armies of Israel, whom you have defied' (verse 45). And the Philistine clanked towards him covered in brass. David ran. Accustomed to rough ground he would have had no problem crossing the brook and negotiating the stones and pebbles along its banks. He had picked up five of them. He was a good judge of stones — their weight, their size and their smoothness for accurate slinging. Not for nothing had he been guarding his father's sheep, perfecting his skills in keeping wild beasts at bay and learning how bulk cancels out agility. Perhaps Goliath had lifted his helmet in disbelief at so youthful an adversary and it was then that David saw his chance. He put his hand in his bag, drew out a stone and 'slung it'. He did not miss. He never missed. The stone sank into the giant's forehead and felled him.

'So David prevailed over the Philistine with a sling and with a stone, and struck the Philistine, and killed him; but there was no sword in the hand of David.'

★   ★   ★

'Five smooth stones' — what paltry ammunition with which to slay a giant! And one of them only sufficed. What we must remember is that they had been selected by an expert: they were for slinging by an expert. Whatever deeper lessons this story may convey it underlies the importance of expertise. David did nothing by halves. And he wasted no opportunities, making use of his time as a shepherd in the wilds to perfect his skills with a sling and studying the habits of wild beasts until he knew exactly how and when to bring a dangerous one down with a stone accurately slung. So David killed Goliath through his expertise. This is the lesson. Giants are not defeated without techniques patiently acquired.

This point needs emphasis because too readily David's religious commitment is counted as the source of his success. That he had a living faith in God the story makes clear, and certainly without the faith he would never have risked his life to face Goliath. But faith alone did not win the battle. Faith and expertise operated here; faith and works. David was a God-fearing youth *and* a skilled youth; the two together made him the giant on the field of battle that day, if not in physical stature, certainly in accomplishment throughout the whole of his life.

So in the contests of life — and they come to us all — we ought not to reckon that the victory must of necessity go to the strong. Nor in debates must the truth always lie with the majority. Nor must the Church employ the world's pressure tactics in order to win a hearing. All this is to reckon without God who, as St Paul wrote to the Corinthians (1 Corinthians 1.27), 'chose what is weak in the world to shame the strong. God chose what is low and despised in the world, even the things that are not, to bring to nothing things that are, so that no human being might boast in the presence of God'. St Paul may well have learnt this lesson from reading the story of the five smooth stones. And so, too, we are reminded of our obligations to devote our own time and skills to God, to withstand provocative insults and resist powerful giants — whoever, or whatever, they might be.

29

Disposer supreme, and Judge of the earth,
Who choosest for thine the meek and the poor;
To frail earthen vessels, and things of no worth,
Entrusting thy riches which ay shall endure.

J.B. de Santeuil, translated by I. Williams

Prayer

Lord, your Church has its giants to fight,
    materialism,
    hedonism,
    rationalism,
    mocking the apparent simplicity of our faith.
Grant us the wisdom to out-think our opponents,
    to keep our nerve for the contest,
    and to remember that the battle is yours
    and that you give power to the faint.
We pray in the name of him who was called
    the Son of David,
    Jesus Christ our Lord.

Beyond sentiment

[31]And behold, the Cushite came; and the Cushite said, 'Good tidings for my lord the king! For the Lord has delivered you this day from the power of all who rose up against you'. [32]The king said to the Cushite, 'Is it well with the young man Absalom?' And the Cushite answered, 'May the enemies of my lord the king, and all who rise up against you for evil, be like that young man'. [33]And the king was deeply moved, and went up to the chamber over the gate, and wept; and as he went, he said, 'O my son Absalom, my son, my son Absalom! Would I had died instead of you, O Absalom, my son, my son!'

2 Samuel 18.31−33 (RSV)

You are looking at an old man. Forget that he is a king. In the present situation he has forgotten it himself. He is a father in whom sentiment has overridden wisdom. You see him sitting between Mahanaim's city gates, having been sitting there ever since he reviewed his troops marching to battle. Two concerns have been dominating his thinking the whole day long; the battle raging in the forest of Ephraim and his rebellious son, on whom he doted, in the thick of it. His son was the commander of the rebel army out there, but what chance had they against his own troops? Thousands would be slain, many of his own faithful soldiers. But for them he showed no concern; all his thoughts were for his wayward, flashy son.

When the message came that 'the Lord has delivered you this day from the power of all who rose up against you', there was no flicker of relief in King David's tired face. Fearful of the answer, he nevertheless urgently put the only question that blotted everything else out: 'Is it well with the young man Absalom?' But the eyes of the messenger did not soften. In biting tones he all but shouted, 'May the enemies of my lord the king, and all who rise up against you for evil, *be like that young man*'. David turned from his place by the gate to climb the stairs crying with every painful step, 'O my son Absalom, my son, my son Absalom! Would I had died instead of you, O Absalom, my son, my son!'

An observer of this scene of broken-heartedness would have to be made of stone not to be moved by it. Let it be granted that David's sentimental attachment to Absalom had got the better of him. Let it be granted that in his ignominious death (2 Samuel 18.9—18), Absalom had received no more than he deserved. And let it be granted that Absalom had to some extent become the vain and conceited upstart he was because his father had spoiled him. Nevertheless, grief is grief, and there are few sights more hurting than an ageing man, crumpled up and tears streaming down his lined face.

However, where are the limitations of such sentiment? Where there is love and bereavement strikes, there is descent into heartbreak, but in the mists of the heart's excusable misery there lurks a fatal danger — self-pity — and if this hardens into self-centredness there is no more certain way of losing the love of those who stand by, multiplying the loss. David's love for Absalom had fallen into this trap and had become the kind of sentiment which no one can admire. It was only at a stinging remark by Joab that David was eventually brought back to the gate of Mahanaim to express the appreciation he had forgotten he owed to those who preserved his throne.

★　　★　　★

Although this picture is a moving one, let us look beyond the sentiment to the deeper message. Firstly we can see a far from outdated dilemma concerning values and loyalties. Here is a couple defiantly defending their daughter who has been flagrantly disloyal to the organization with whom she has signed an undertaking of absolute discretion. Here is a mother quick to condemn the widespread incidence of divorce but her son who is divorced has done no wrong. Here is a smart young 'man about town' caught with illicit drugs but according to his family it is his 'set' who have led him astray; he himself is innocent. Is it possible for relatives to see straight about the misdemeanours of their own people? In such dilemmas, where do our loyalties lie, and where should they lie?

There is another message. David wept over Absalom, the son who did not merely ask but sought to take by force what he reckoned should be his. But David loved him. So, too, God loves us — rebellious humanity; metaphorically speaking, he, too, weeps over us and our sorry world. But God's love is not sentimental. There is judgement in it, and we distort the truth if ever we present God as a sentimental aged grandfather. God's love is demanding; it saves, but at a price.

Prayer

> Lord, deliver me from self-centredness
> when I an unwell,
> when I am disappointed,
> when I am sad, even heart-broken.
> Let me remember that neither grief nor love
> is sentiment alone.
> I need your grace to take me beyond.

Still small voice

[9]And there he came to a cave, and lodged there; and behold, the word of the Lord came to him, and he said to him, 'What are you doing here, Elijah?' [10]He said, 'I have been very jealous for the Lord, the God of hosts; for the people of Israel have forsaken thy covenant, thrown down thy altars, and slain thy prophets with the sword; and I, even I only, am left; and they seek my life, to take it away'. [11]And he said, 'Go forth, and stand upon the mount before the Lord'. And behold, the Lord passed by, and a great and strong wind rent the mountains, and broke in pieces the rocks before the Lord, but the Lord was not in the wind; and after the wind an earthquake, but the Lord was not in the earthquake; [12]and after the earthquake a fire, but the Lord was not in the fire; and after the fire a still small voice. [13]And when Elijah heard it, he wrapped his face in his mantle and went out and stood at the entrance of the cave. And behold, there came a voice to him, and said, 'What are you doing here, Elijah?' [14]He said, 'I have been very jealous for the Lord, the God of hosts; for the people of Israel have forsaken thy covenant, thrown down thy altars, and slain thy prophets with the sword; and I, even I only, am left; and they seek my life, to take it away'. [15]And the Lord said to him, 'Go, return on your way to the wilderness of Damascus; and when you arrive, you shall anoint Hazael to be king over Syria; [16]and Jehu the son of Nimshi you shall anoint to be king over Israel; and Elisha the son of Shaphat of Abelmeholah you shall anoint to be prophet in your place'.

1 Kings 19.9—16 (RSV)

You find yourself staring at a wild, hideously ferocious aspect of nature in this picture. Precipitous rock faces, jagged and broken, with here and there a dark and mysterious cave; a wind rising, tearing, a terrifying precursor of a violent storm; and thunder reverberating around the mountains, flashing them into vivid brightness every now and again with blue-forked lightning reaching down to splinter the rocks and hurtle them into the ravine below. The whole place shaken with an earthquake. And there, high up on an all but inaccessible ledge, you see a gaunt and exhausted figure, struggling to stand against the fierceness of the elements, his face wrapped in his cloak. It is Elijah, the man whose whole ministry was conducted in a torment of energy forever wrestling against the odds, be it the fickleness of King Ahab, the cruel cunning of Queen Jezebel or the dull plodding religious unbelief of the majority of their subjects. And now he feels himself finished. There was no more that he could do, no more that he could give. He had played himself out in the fierce contest with the priests of Baal on Mount Carmel and then fled to the desert in fear, there to sink exhausted under a juniper tree pleading with God for death as a merciful way out of the battle. But death did not come, so now you see him up on Mount Horeb — the place where Moses received the divine commandments — his whole life, as he thought, shattered like the scene before him.

Back in the cave, however, in one of those moments of breathtaking silence that so often interpose themselves between the crashes of thunder, he heard, as it were, a 'still small voice' calling to his inner being. Was it natural for a man of Elijah's stamp to recognize God's presence, God's action and God's voice in the cataclysms of human history and the terrorizing upheavals of his environment, God coming there with loud clarion calls to heed his commandments? But in the storm raging across Horeb as he cowered in his cave Elijah heard nothing: 'The Lord was not in the wind . . . the Lord was not in the earthquake'. But God was in the 'still small voice'.

★　　★　　★

Is this the lesson this sensational picture has been painted to teach us? Is this the lesson Elijah needed to learn? God comes in the stillness. He is present in the ordinary and commonplace, as well as at times in the spectacular. Elijah had wanted to see smashing victories in God's service casting down the wickedness of humanity. Who doesn't? And Elijah wished to be in the thick of the fight himself. But this is not how God necessarily works; he works slowly, and patiently, and in quiet ways drawing on men and women with the constraints of his love, not with the fury of his anger.

Twice in that cave Elijah had cried aloud his endeavours on behalf of God. 'I have been very jealous for the Lord, the God of hosts'. And God, as it were, said, 'Yes I know, but go and carry out this piece of "admin" work will you? Make Hazael king of Syria and Jehu king of Israel and anoint Elisha to take your place.' But how dull! How ordinary and unheroic! Surely this shows us that God

works through the routine as well as through the exceptional, situations in life.

When we are assailed from all sides by turbulent circumstances,
we can be reassured that eventually calm will descend — the still
small voice. Whatever danger — real or imaginary — is happening
at this moment *it will pass* and we will be safe in the hands
of God.

Prayer

> Drop thy still dews of quietness,
> Till all our strivings cease;
> Take from our souls the strain and stress,
> And let our ordered lives confess
> The beauty of thy peace.
>
> Breathe through the heats of our desire
> Thy coolness and thy balm;
> Let sense be dumb, let flesh retire;
> Speak through the earthquake, wind, and fire,
> O still small voice of calm!

J.G. Whittier

New beginnings

2 Now when the Lord was about to take Elijah up to heaven by a whirlwind, Elijah and Elisha were on their way from Gilgal . . . ⁴Elijah said to
him, 'Elisha, tarry here, I pray you; for the Lord has sent me to Jericho'.
But he said, 'As the Lord lives, and as you yourself live, I will not leave
you'. So they came to Jericho. ⁵The sons of the prophets who were at
Jericho drew near to Elisha, and said to him, 'Do you know that today
the Lord will take away your master from over you?' And he answered,
'Yes, I know it; hold your peace'.

⁶Then Elijah said to him, 'Tarry here, I pray you; for the Lord has sent me to the Jordan'. But he said, 'As the Lord lives, and as you yourself live, I will not leave you'. ⁷So the two of them went on. Fifty men of the sons of the prophets also went, and stood at some distance from them, as they both were standing by the Jordan. ⁸Then Elijah took his mantle, and rolled it up, and struck the water, and the water was parted to the one side and to the other, till the two of them could go over on dry ground.

⁹When they had crossed, Elijah said to Elisha, 'Ask what I shall do for you, before I am taken from you'. And Elisha said, 'I pray you, let me inherit a double share of your spirit'. ¹⁰And he said, 'You have asked a hard thing; yet, if you see me as I am being taken from you, it shall be so for you; but if you do not see me, it shall not be so'. ¹¹And as they still went on and talked, behold, a chariot of fire and horses of fire separated the two of them. And Elijah went up by a whirlwind into heaven. ¹²And Elisha saw it and he cried, 'My father, my father! The chariots of Israel and its horsemen!' And he saw him no more.

Then he took hold of his own clothes and rent them in two pieces. ¹³And he took up the mantle of Elijah that had fallen from him, and went back and stood on the bank of the Jordan. ¹⁴Then he took the mantle of Elijah that had fallen from him, and struck the water, saying 'Where is the Lord, the God of Elijah?' And when he had struck the water, the water was parted to the one side and to the other; and Elisha went over.

¹⁵Now when the sons of the prophets who were at Jericho saw him over against them, they said, 'The spirit of Elijah rests on Elisha'. And they came to meet him, and bowed to the ground before him.

2 Kings 2, selected verses (RSV)

Elijah's death must come soon, but Elisha dreaded it. Perhaps he had become aware of his master's failing powers for some time. But old men with vigorous minds do not readily surrender nor slough off the marks of their former vigour. Not surprisingly, therefore, Elijah kept his sturdy independence to the end; but the end had to come and that soon. Death was at hand, but Elijah was determined to face it alone.

Elisha read the signs but was taken aback when his master resolutely announced his intention of travelling to Jericho at the Lord's command and that he, Elisha, was not to accompany him; but Elisha insisted. So they arrived at Jericho where the students in the local prophetic seminary insensitively whispered the obvious to Elisha, 'Do you know that today the Lord will take away your master from over you?' They need not have been surprised when Elisha, taut with impending bereavement, curtly told them to hold their peace. There are parts of life which must be suffered in silence.

The Jordan river was not far away and Elijah was determined to press on to it alone. But Elisha protested once again, so they went together, the sons of the prophets (whoever they were) standing at a distance to watch. They saw Elijah remove his cloak, strike the waters with it and cross the river, perhaps at a ford they knew. On the other side, Elijah spoke plainly to his almost heart-broken follower. 'Ask what I shall do for you, before I am taken from you'. Did a long pause follow? Then Elisha asked for 'a double share' of Elijah's spirit — an endowment twice that granted to most prophets (although he was not asking to be twice the man his master was). It was such a hard request since no one can bestow his spiritual endowment on anyone else; only God can bestow his spirit as he wills.

So Elijah answered evasively, 'If you see me as I am being taken from you it shall be so for you; but if you do not see me it shall not be so.' They toiled up to the higher ground, talking as they went. Then, all at once, an horrendous storm broke. Elijah was not unfamiliar with storms: he had faced storms of one kind or another all his life, and had survived them — but not this time. It was to be his last. Elisha saw him go. There were no traces left, only his cloak. Dazed, at last Elisha found the strength to pick up that cloak and make his way back and down to the river Jordan using it to cross the waters as he had seen his master do so. The sons of the prophets at Jericho watched from afar. Seeing Elisha returning alone, they said, 'The spirit of Elijah rests on Elisha'. Then, daring to venture to meet him, they bowed themselves to the ground. A new prophetic era had begun. God's power was still to be manifest.

★   ★   ★

Can there be any comments apt for this dramatic scene? None, maybe, unless and until we have been forced to watch the life of someone of full age, someone to whom we are devoted, slowly but surely ebb away. We know the end has to come and we dread its coming; yet we would not wish to stop it if we could, because the time has come, the life has run its appointed course. But the process of ending is melancholy and often anguished. We begin to sense the ensuing emptiness and to wonder if our own existence can con-

tinue meaningfully, because to a large extent we live through the
people we love. Our grief will be intense; periods of depression and
despondency may well follow. Our feelings may be numbed. This
picture, however, tells us how to begin to live again. We can eventually release our inner sorrows and God will give us the strength to
use our sufferings creatively. We can start again: take up the mantle. Continue the work and witness of goodness our departed loved
ones were forced to lay down, even if we happen to be a very
different kind of person in temperament and in style, even as Elisha
with his quiet, steady effectiveness differed from Elijah, and his
energetic ministry. Remember that God works in his world
through the quiescent Elishas as well as through the forceful
Elijahs.

Prayer

> Jesus, still lead on,
> Till our rest be won,
> And, although the way be cheerless,
> We will follow calm and fearless;
> Guide us by thy hand
> To our Fatherland.

Count N.L. Zinzendorf
Translated by Jane L. Borthwick

Pocketed pride

5 Naaman, commander of the army of the king of Syria, was a great
man with his master and in high favour, because by him the Lord had
given victory to Syria. He was a mighty man of valour, but he was a
leper. ²Now the Syrians on one of their raids had carried off a little
maid from the land of Israel, and she waited on Naaman's wife. ³She

said to her mistress, 'Would that my lord were with the prophet who is in Samaria! He would cure him of his leprosy'. So Naaman went in and told his lord, 'Thus and so spoke the maiden from the land of Israel'. And the king of Syria said, 'Go now, and I will send a letter to the king of Israel'.

So he went, taking with him ten talents of silver, six thousand shekels of gold, and ten festal garments. ⁶And he brought the letter to the king of Israel, which read, 'When this letter reaches you, know that I have sent to you Naaman my servant, that you may cure him of his leprosy'. ⁷And when the king of Israel read the letter, he rent his clothes and said, 'Am I God, to kill and to make alive, that this man sends word to me to cure a man of his leprosy? Only consider, and see how he is seeking a quarrel with me'.

⁸But when Elisha the man of God heard that the king of Israel had rent his clothes, he sent to the king, saying, 'Why have you rent your clothes? Let him come now to me, that he may know that there is a prophet in Israel'. ⁹So Naaman came with his horses and chariots, and halted at the door of Elisha's house. ¹⁰And Elisha sent a messenger to him, saying, 'Go and wash in the Jordan seven times, and your flesh shall be restored, and you shall be clean'. ¹¹But Naaman was angry, and went away, saying, 'Behold, I thought that he would surely come out to me, and stand, and call on the name of the Lord his God, and wave his hand over the place, and cure the leper. ¹²Are not Abana and Pharpar, the rivers of Damascus, better than all the waters of Israel? Could I not wash in them, and be clean?' So he turned and went away in a rage. ¹³But his servants came near and said to him, 'My father, if the prophet had commanded you to do some great thing, would you not have done it? How much rather, then, when he says to you, "Wash, and be clean"?' ¹⁴So he went down and dipped himself seven times in the Jordan, according to the word of the man of God; and his flesh was restored like the flesh of a little child, and he was clean.

2 Kings 5.1—14 (RSV)

Before all else notice what a great man this Naaman was — great in the eyes of his Syrian countrymen, great in the eyes of his king, great, we perceive in his own eyes, considering all this public esteem. But this literary masterpiece — and it certainly is that, fourteen verses only and everything essential told in fast-moving prose alive with direct speech — offers a glaring contrast. A great man, yes, but also a little girl and she the key figure. No one could be less great, as girls were of little account in that culture. But the story turns on her. Without 'the little maid' there would be no story.

For all their lofty state, their wealth and their correspondence, neither the king of Syria nor the king of Israel could meet the great man's need of healing from the damaging skin disease, leprosy. Naaman has to step down to a man of religion; in fact, to Elisha, 'the man of God' in Israel of whom 'the little maid' with touching concern for her magnificent master had spoken to her mistress. But when Naaman did step down, Elisha did not stand to attention. There was no face to face meeting. The great man, Naaman, was given instructions by an intermediary. 'Go and wash in the Jordan seven times.' Not surprisingly, Naaman felt insulted, having been cut down to the size of a commonplace patient. He stormed about the place. But this was not the only humiliation. Just as a slave girl had initiated the visit to Elisha so, too, his slave retinue had to calm him down. 'If the prophet had commanded you do some great thing, would you not have done it?' How well they knew their man! The great man would certainly do great things. But he was merely invited to do a little thing — dip in the River Jordan. Grudgingly he went, and, like a common pilgrim, dipped seven times in the Jordan, a mere stream compared to the great rivers of Damascus he knew so well. There was to be no sudden magic cure with the movement of the prophet's hand, nothing on which to hold but a *word*, the word of the man of God.

The outstanding feature of this masterpiece, then, is the stark contrast of greatness and littleness; we have before us a colourful reminder of the sovereignty of God.

> Yours, Lord, is the greatness, the power,
> the glory, the splendour, and the majesty;
> for everything in heaven and on earth is yours.
> All things come from you,
> and of your own do we give you.

ASB Holy Communion, Rite A

The story of Naaman cuts us down to size with respect to our faith. Salvation is not conditioned by the amount of what we have. Was any faith so little as that which Naaman exercised? Yet he was cured of his leprosy. In effect he said to himself, 'It is a paltry action that I am asked to perform, and little is the faith I have in it, but it can do no harm. It is at least worth the gamble'. On that flimsiest of faith he came up out of the River Jordan a clean man, cleansed of his malady.

Again, we are reminded of our rational limitations when confronted by the enormity of God. Human progress in the arts and sciences, particularly the latter, has been monumental in the last two centuries. Nevertheless, we cannot think our way to God. We cannot even prove his existence: we may claim to see signs of his presence, or may affirm that we have heard his word, but at the end of the day we have to admit that what we profess is faith not knowledge, however rigorously we maintain that our faith is not unreasonable. Rather than submit to the concept of this inadequacy of human reason some thinkers dismiss the idea of God altogether. No, we do not enjoy being cut down to size in the sphere of our mental faculties.

★   ★   ★

As we look at all the details in this picture, we gradually realize that we are all like Naaman; the whole human race is like Naaman, including you and me. For all our apparent prowess we suffer in some degree from the contagiousness of universal pride though we hate to admit it. We need cleansing. Human salvation is not a state we can *achieve* either by intellect or by faith; it can only be received, for it is a gift of God to whom he chooses, and for reasons beyond our capacity to unravel. All we can do is obey the word of God as it comes to us, often in a humble, even pedestrian form. Naaman heard the word of God through Elisha behind a closed door repeated by a servant. Healing begins at the place where we are willing to hear God's command, to obey it, and to go down in submission to God as sovereign lord who nevertheless cares for us. This simple gospel is the message which the story of Naaman, the great man, and 'the little maid', is artistically constructed to convey. The great and the small among us would be wise to remember it.

Prayer

> So, Lord, I must pocket my pride,
>   my pride of intellect,
>   my pride of religion,
>   my pride of achievement.
> I must hear your word,
>   obey your word,
>   and be willing humbly to receive it.

I find this hard, Lord.
I want to make myself acceptable,
    acceptable to you,
    acceptable to my friends.
And I shall be if I receive what you offer.
Give me grace to believe this,
    to act upon it,
    and to know the joy of acceptance.
By you, the sovereign Lord of all,
through Jesus Christ our Lord.

God's repairer

---

¹¹Now I was cupbearer to the king. **2** In the month of Nisan, in the twentieth year of King Artaxerxes, when wine was before him, I took up the wine and gave it to the king. Now I had not been sad in his presence. ²And the king said to me, 'Why is your face sad, seeing you are not sick? This is nothing else but sadness of the heart'. Then I was very much afraid. ³I said to the king, 'Let the king live for ever! Why should not my face be sad, when the city, the place of my fathers' sepulchres, lies waste, and its gates have been destroyed by fire?' ⁴Then the king said to me, 'For what do you make request?' So I prayed to the God of heaven. ⁵And I said to the king, 'If it pleases the king, and if your servant has found favour in your sight, that you send me to Judah, to the city of my fathers' sepulchres, that I may rebuild it'. ⁶And the king said to me (the queen sitting beside him), 'How long will you be gone, and when will you return?' So it pleased the king to send me; and I set him a time. ⁷And I said to the king, 'If it pleases the king, let letters be given me to the governors of the province Beyond the River, that they may let me pass through until I come to Judah; ⁸and a letter to Asaph, the keeper of the king's forest, that he may give me timber to make beams for the gates of the fortress of the temple, and for the wall of the city, and for the house which I shall occupy'. And the king granted me what I asked, for the good hand of my God was upon me.

Nehemiah 1.11—2.8 (RSV)

In this picture, we meet Nehemiah, a man who gives the impression of being intelligent, with *savoir faire*, polish and charm. He has not been made the king's cupbearer for nothing; the cupbearer was not a kind of wine waiter at royal banquets but, if not exactly the prime minister as in our democratic constitution, yet the first among the king's advisers in the business of governing the country. This accounts for the king's reluctance to allow him prolonged absence from the court.

Alexander Whyte, the Scottish preacher, in one of his books tells a story based upon Josephus, the first-century Jewish historian, which, if it is not true, we feel ought to be. Nehemiah was taking the air one night outside the walls of Persepolis when some travel-stained men passed him on their way to the city gates. He heard them speaking to each other in their mother tongue, Hebrew. Prosperous though he was, beautiful clothes and all, the sound struck his heart with longing. He had to stop them to enquire after the state of Jerusalem, and what he heard saddened him. He could not banish the dismal report from his mind, not even when he had reached the top level of society, moving freely in the royal circles to which he had grown accustomed. Always he saw in his mind's eye Jerusalem, his mother city, still in ruins after the devastation of the Babylonian conquest.

The scene in front of us depicts a day when at a banquet King Artaxerxes observed the sad demeanour of his chief adviser, Nehemiah, and enquired the reason. Nehemiah sensed danger, not least because the queen was sitting by him, able to whisper in his ear. A powerful woman in the kingdom, she was not slow to influence the king in ways suitable to her wishes, sometimes with ruthless consequences. Nehemiah had to divulge the reason for his sadness — a personal concern about his devastated native land. The king sensed an unspoken request and wished to know what it was.

We can visualize Nehemiah at that moment holding his breath. This might be the occasion of his fall from grace. Was he asking too much? Absolute rulers are known to act on impulses. So Nehemiah prayed to the God of heaven. It was what we call an 'arrow prayer', a sudden lifting up of the heart to God in time of need. Daringly he proceeded with his request to return to Judah where he could rebuild Jerusalem. He spoke with becoming deference. Twice over he had referred to his 'fathers' sepulchres' suggesting a mission of filial piety likely to appeal perhaps to the king. It did so, for he enquired when Nehemiah would return and a time was set. Encouraged, therefore, Nehemiah asked for royal letters to expedite his passage through the territory on the journey to Jerusalem, and even for a letter to the keeper of the king's forest to grant him wood for the repairs he would undertake. All was agreed and Nehemiah in the secret of his heart gave thanks to God to whose good hand he attributed this astonishing success.

So we see Nehemiah departing from this picture to accomplish with astonishing energy the repair work on Jerusalem's city walls, to inspire others and to resist those who sought to oppose him.

★   ★   ★

Within this frame a secular environment is painted, yet one which conveys a religious end. In the Old Testament gallery we see time and again that God is both *holy*, beyond and above human affairs, and that he is *immanent*, in the very midst of his people, guiding them and operating through their lives. The sacred and secular are woven into a single context. We tend to have a very different approach today, often managing to segregate our spiritual lives from our daily chores, thus failing to see God in everyday situations. Indeed, we frequently have preconceived ideas of what a 'religious person' must look like, or what kind of jobs they ought to be doing. But the picture of Nehemiah may help us to look beneath the surface and beyond our conventional expectations.

Prayer

> Lord, you have placed me where I am in the world
> for some good purpose.
> Most of what I do is not religious work;
> most of my time I cannot be thinking of you;
> most often I have to keep my faith to myself.
> But I am a believer,
> a believer in your presence,
> a believer in your care for me,
> one to whom I can turn
> when the going gets tough.

And when things turn out well as they often do,
give me grace then to return to you in thanksgiving
for your good hand upon me,
I pray in the name of Jesus Christ our Lord.

Powerful worship

6 In the year that King Uzziah died I saw the Lord sitting upon a throne, high and lifted up; and his train filled the temple. [2] Above him stood the seraphim; each had six wings: with two he covered his face, and with two he covered his feet, and with two he flew. [3] And one called to another and said: 'Holy, holy, holy is the Lord of hosts; the whole earth is full of his glory'. [4] And the foundations of the thresholds shook at the voice of him who called, and the house was filled with smoke. [5] And I said: 'Woe is me! For I am lost; for I am a man of unclean lips, and I dwell in the midst of a people of unclean lips, for my eyes have seen the King, the Lord of hosts!'

[6] Then flew one of the seraphim to me, having in his hand a burning coal which he had taken with tongs from the altar. [7] And he touched my mouth, and said: 'Behold, this has touched your lips; your guilt is taken away, and your sin forgiven'. [8] And I heard the voice of the Lord saying, 'Whom shall I send, and who will go for us?' Then I said, 'Here am I! Send me'.

Isaiah 6.1–8 (RSV)

I remember an occasion, about fifty years ago, when I found myself for the first time in St Paul's Cathedral in London, listening to a recital of Handel's *Messiah* conducted as an act of worship. Having been brought up in an ordinary seaside town, I was spellbound by the majestic splendour of that magnificent building. The music and beauty of surroundings lifted me clean out of myself. Clearly this act of worship did something to me and I knew it. I had been touched by the Transcendent. And that to my mind is what worship should do for us — touch us with the Transcendent, what Rudolf Otto — a well-known German theologian concerned with the nature of religious experience — called an 'above the world' experience.

Now the vision portrayed in this vivid scene might be expected to stand at the beginning of Isaiah's book representing the occasion of his call to his prophetic ministry, but, in fact, it is held back until Chapter 6. Prior to it, a picture of worship is indeed displayed — packed services, crowds of worshippers, people falling over themselves to bring their offerings. To furnish God with human emotions, we can well imagine him as it were sitting up in heaven exasperated with this worship, his fingers in his ears, his eyes tight shut and crying out, 'I can't stand any more of it!' Or as the scripture has it, 'I am weary of bearing them'. Such was the worship Isaiah had endured for years, and the people associated with it were besotted with two inflamed desires: the urge to acquire and the urge to dissipate, in a word money and drink. This is made explicit in Isaiah 5.8—23, the immediate preface to Isaiah's vision of the Transcendent in Chapter 6.

So, wearied with this glut of superficial religion cloaking the coarseness, indeed callousness, of current conduct, Isaiah fell to brooding. How hopes for the nation had been lifted up when young King Uzziah had ascended the throne! What chances there were for the future! But how did it end? How did Uzziah end? In a house ridden with leprosy (2 Chronicles 26). And when the news leaked out that Uzziah at last had died, Isaiah sat contemplating all this melancholy history. Then it was that the vision stood out sharp and clear before his consciousness — 'In the year that King Uzziah died I saw the Lord, sitting upon a throne, high and lifted up; and his train filled the temple'.

The instinctive response of Isaiah in the face of such glory was to confess: 'I am lost; for I am a man of unclean lips, and I dwell in the midst of a people of unclean lips; for my eyes have seen the King, the Lord of Hosts!' Overwhelmed by the mystery and power of God, Isaiah suddenly became aware of how small he was, and how lost his people were so long as they reckoned that they controlled their own destiny. The truth is that not Uzziah, nor Isaiah, nor, for us, democracy, or the EEC, is the Lord of history, but he who sits on the throne whose presence can strike like thunder but whom we only half see. And when we can apprehend this reality God's presence will cleanse us immediately, like the burning coal which touches Isaiah's lips and instantly removes his guilt.

★   ★   ★

It is unlikely that we shall ever have a dramatic vision of the Lord and certainly not every Sunday. For many of us, however, there may be sharp, intense occasions, when perhaps we have come to the end of ourselves and our human resources, and when we cry out, 'God I'm finished! I'm through! But you, Lord, are on the throne; I'm in your hands!' Bereavement, failure, an unexpected success, perhaps an answer to prayer about the apparently impossible: these are the times when an experience of a transcending, even visionary, nature can happen. Granted, such occasions are rare, but they are the kind of markers that can indicate the pattern of worship over and against which all our acts of worship may be measured. Such disclosure points of the Transcendent allow the curtains to be drawn aside for a moment so that we may see God reigning in our own personal history.

Now let us look more carefully at the picture before us. There is grandeur; a throne; a palace; angelic attendants around the throne; a heavenly choir, one side chanting, 'Holy, holy, holy', the other side replying 'The whole earth is full of his glory'. So glory illumi nates the whole picture. And if our worship is to convey a sense of the transcendent and immense holiness of God then there must be some grandeur about it — however it may be expressed — through scripture, music or ritual. Worship should aim to touch us — to uplift and refresh our spirits. Moreover, as this picture reminds us, worship is never an end in itself. We should 'go in peace to love and serve the Lord'. Worshippers have a task to perform; Isaiah with his peculiar gifts, you with yours, I with mine. 'Here am I! Send me'.

Confession

We praise thee, O God: we acknowledge thee to be the Lord.
All the earth doth worship thee: the Father everlasting.

From the Te Deum, Book of Common Prayer

Unstable foundations

³¹'You saw, O king, and behold, a great image. This image, mighty and of exceeding brightness, stood before you, and its appearance was frightening. ³²The head of this image was of fine gold, its breast and arms of silver, its belly and thighs of bronze, ³³its legs of iron, its feet partly of iron and partly of clay. ³⁴As you looked, a stone was cut out by no human hand, and it smote the image on its feet of iron and clay, and broke them in pieces; ³⁵then the iron, the clay, the bronze, the silver, and the gold, all together were broken in pieces, and became like the chaff of the summer threshing floors; and the wind carried them away, so that not a trace of them could be found. But the stone that struck the image became a great mountain and filled the whole earth.'

Daniel 2.31—35 (RSV)

We see in this picture what Nebuchadnezzar, King of Babylon, saw in his dream, and which kept him awake at night, troubling him in the following days, as well it might for it struck at the whole of his imagined strength and security. He saw a mighty threatening image which nevertheless stood on fragile feet. Could it possibly be that the day would dawn when his powerful and extensive kingdom would be shattered and lie in ruins, a thing of the past over which men would shake their heads? He must be told what this dream signified.

But would his magicians, enchanters and sorcerers ever divulge to him that terrible forecast even if they knew it? Their lives were in the king's blood-stained hands as are all lives under the rule of a military dictator. Nevertheless, they said to the king, 'Tell us the dream and we will show you the interpretation'. But the suspicious king required that they first tell him what he had dreamed then he would know they could provide the interpretation. All this under pain of death. Not surprisingly they complained that this was an impossible condition and paid the ultimate penalty. Nebuchadnezzar's rule was indeed built on a basis of terror.

So Daniel, the Jewish exile, with his reputation for wisdom was summoned. He fulfilled the requirements: he told the king his dream and provided the interpretation (vv. 36—45). Nebuchadnezzar's kingdom, represented by the golden head of the mighty image, would be succeeded by three other kingdoms, one of silver, one of bronze and one of iron. All four, however, would be found to be resting on feet made of iron and clay, substances which do not bind together and provide stability. Therefore, all would totter and fall. God who is over all kingdoms would be the agent of the fall and he would set up a kingdom to stand for ever. This is what the future holds.

Here we encounter a class of literary material very different from what much of the Bible holds, though it does crop up in various places most notably in the book of Revelation or the Apocalypse. It is called 'apocalyptic' which means an uncovering of what is hidden, that is to say, it is a revelation of the future. Full of symbolic and visual imagery, it certainly catches our attention, but we need to be careful not to reject this material out of hand as narrow and sectarian. The book of Daniel, in fact, unlike a great part of the Bible, looks beyond Israel, the 'chosen people', to events on the world stage. Furthermore, what this 'image dream' in particular provides is a diagnosis of the fatal weakness which lies at the basis of proud world powers. They will not in consequence last.

*   *   *

Sadly, the twentieth century has provided many examples of leaders attempting to exercise absolute power and manipulating other nations. This picture shows that such power will not last — it has unstable foundations. There is also a warning here for the Western democracies drifting further and further away from their traditional moral foundation with little or no attempt to recover it. Democracy does not of itself produce a moral framework; it must be found elsewhere, in the hearts and minds and actions of individuals. Nations emerging from communism will need to learn this also. In a vivid way, apocalyptic can remind us of the dangers of putting our trust too heavily in worldly powers and external structures. Stable foundations begin from within ourselves.

Prayer

> Almighty and everlasting God, in whose power lie
> all the kingdoms of men, grant unto all in authority

in our land such humility of mind as becomes those
who exercise their leadership on trust from thee
that our security be not jeopardized through
overwhelming pride.
We ask in the name of Jesus Christ our Lord.

THE NEW TESTAMENT

St Matthew's Christmas story

[18]Now the birth of Jesus Christ took place in this way. When his mother Mary had been betrothed to Joseph, before they came together she was found to be with child of the Holy Spirit; [19]and her husband Joseph, being a just man and unwilling to put her to shame, resolved to divorce her quietly. [20]But as he considered this, behold, an angel of the Lord appeared to him in a dream, saying, 'Joseph, son of David, do not fear to take Mary your wife, for that which is conceived in her is of the Holy Spirit; [21]she will bear a son, and you shall call his name Jesus, for he will save his people from their sins'. [22]All this took place to fulfil what the Lord had spoken by the prophet:

[23]'Behold, a virgin shall conceive and bear a son,
and his name shall be called Emmanuel'

(which means, God with us). [24]When Joseph woke from sleep, he did as the angel of the Lord commanded him; he took his wife, [25]but knew her not until she had borne a son; and he called his name Jesus.

Matthew 1.18—25 (RSV)

As we view this Christmas picture we have to take a firm grip on ourselves if we are to appreciate it. Here is Christmas without the baby in the manger, without the shepherds 'abiding in the fields keeping watch over their flocks by night', without the heavenly host chanting 'Glory to God in the highest'. We have to remind ourselves that before the New Testament was constituted as we have it now with its four gospels two of them, St Matthew and St Luke, telling of Jesus' birth, some churches only had the one gospel which was written primarily for them. Such was St Matthew's gospel most likely written for some early Jewish-Christian church possibly in Syria. What then did its readers come to know about the birth of Jesus with no other gospel before them? This is the question to keep before us as we study the picture St Matthew has provided.

Most vividly they learned about Joseph who dominates the scene. What they, and we, are made to see is a distracted man, terribly distracted, pacing, maybe, up and down his room in the evenings, after work, unable to settle, perhaps off his food, sitting at table, his head in his hands, and at night unable to sleep. And all because of Mary, the girl he loved as no one else in all the world, nor ever would. They were engaged to be married in a ceremony which in that community could only be terminated by a legal process. But she was pregnant, not with his child, but God's child, so she implored him to believe — she was still a virgin. Did he believe it? Could he believe it? Would anyone believe it? How many people believe it now? But then, amongst all this unbearable strain, Joseph had a dream which transformed everything; Mary was not deceiving him — all that she had said was true: 'Joseph, son of David, do not fear to take Mary your wife, for that which is conceived in her is of the Holy Spirit; she will bear a son, and you shall call his name Jesus, for he will save his people from their sins'. Such was the message of the angel in his dream.

The clouds of confusion may not have lifted instantly after months of agonizing doubt, but Joseph did as he was 'commanded'; the life which had made no sense was gradually blotted out.

★   ★   ★

And now the question St Matthew's Christmas picture forces us to ask: What kind of world did the author of this gospel wish us to understand that Jesus entered? Can there be any doubt? A world couched in misunderstanding, misapprehension, fear and heart-brokenness. This is our world, the world we all experience in a measure, if not perpetually, yet certainly at times. Jesus was born into this. God in Christ came here. St Matthew stamped it with this extraordinary and unlikely text from Isaiah: 'Behold, a virgin shall conceive and bear a son, and his name shall be called Emmanuel' (Emmanuel meaning, God with us).

Such is the good news of St Matthew's gospel, God with us where we are. We are redeemed because of this. It is the gospel of the incarnation (God taking our flesh upon him) which the Greek Church Fathers preached; the divine mingled in our humanity by the birth of Jesus and saving it. And if our theology centres our redemption on the cross of Christ rather than his birth, let us not fail to hear what St Matthew is proclaiming by means of his Christmas picture which Joseph dominates, poor downcast, distracted Joseph — Emmanuel, God is with us wherever we are.

Prayer

Lord, there have been times when we have not known
    which way to turn;
    this way seems wrong,
    that way seems wrong,
    and we are at our wits end.
Help us, by your grace to believe that
    whichever path we choose
    you will be with us,
    even if it is rough,
    even if it seems to make no sense,
You will never cast us off.
We can go on in this faith
    and the sun will shine again.

Bare essentials

3 In those days came John the Baptist, preaching in the wilderness of Judea, [2]'Repent, for the kingdom of heaven is at hand'. [3]For this is he who was spoken of by the prophet Isaiah when he said,
'The voice of one crying in the wilderness:
Prepare the way of the Lord,
make his paths straight'.
[4]Now John wore a garment of camel's hair, and a leather girdle around his waist; and his food was locusts and wild honey. [5]Then went out to him Jerusalem and all Judea and all the region about the Jordan, [6]and they were baptized by him in the river Jordan, confessing their sins.

Matthew 3.1—6 (RSV)

55

Imagine this whole picture and notice just how crowded the canvas is. Every Tom, Dick and Harry is painted in, and even this will not suffice to indicate the conglomeration, for the small and the great are there, the servant and his master, the labourer and the land-owner, the ruffian and the religious, not to mention the prostitute and her pimp.

But why are they there? The man called John the Baptist, up to his waist in water in the shallows of the River Jordan, holds the key. Look at him: that gaunt figure, those fiery eyes, those accusing pointing fingers when he preaches, and that rough coat of camel's skin with a leather belt to hold it together. No Jew in that crowd could have failed to recognize his resemblance to Elijah, come to life again, ripping off the clothes of his hearers' outward religiosity to reveal the festering hypocrisy beneath. No, they did not like it. They did not like him. But what he said got under their skin. God's day was coming when he would judge his people, and the only way to escape that impending judgement was by means of repentance now, confessing sins and having them washed away in the water of baptism.

It is impossible to approach the beginning of Jesus' ministry in any of the four gospels without first encountering the rather for-midable figure of John the Baptist; his whole life is orientated towards fulfilling his role as the preparer with an urgent message — 'Repent, for the kingdom of heaven is at hand'. The first step in the journey of faith is one of wiping the slate clean, one of transforma-tion: the word for 'to repent' in Greek — *metanoein* — means literally 'to change one's mind', to look at oneself with a new insight, to reorder one's priorities and affirm new principles directed towards God. The process strips us down to the bare essentials, illuminates our sin and draws us into confession.

★　★　★

John the Baptist is out to peel off all the refined or coarse camou-flages by which people hope to hide their lives. Disconcertingly, he keeps on asking what sort of people we are underneath.

Nothing in my hand I bring,
Simply to thy Cross I cling;
Naked, come to thee for dress;
Helpless, look to thee for grace;

Foul, I to the fountain fly;
Wash me, Saviour, or I die.

A.M. Toplady

No wonder we find John the Baptist a formidable figure: through him we are challenged to confront the bare truth about ourselves and our real values. How many layers of different disguises do we have to remove before we are freed from every hypocritical covering? If we want to approach Jesus, we cannot dodge John the Baptist.

Prayer

O Lord Jesus Christ, who at thy first coming didst send thy messenger to prepare thy way before thee: Grant that the ministers and stewards of thy mysteries may likewise so prepare and make ready thy way, by turning the hearts of the disobedient to the wisdom of the just, that at thy second coming to judge the world we may be found an acceptable people in thy sight, who livest and reignest with the Father and the Holy Spirit, ever one God, world without end.

From the Book of Common Prayer

Jesus in the queue

[13]Then Jesus came from Galilee to the Jordan to John, to be baptized by him. [14]John would have prevented him, saying, 'I need to be baptized by you, and do you come to me?' [15]But Jesus answered him, 'Let it be so now; for thus it is fitting for us to fulfil all righteousness'. Then he consented. [16]And when Jesus was baptized, he went up immediately from the water, and behold, the heavens were opened and he saw the Spirit of God descending like a dove, and alighting on him; [17]and lo, a voice from heaven, saying, 'This is my beloved Son, with whom I am well pleased'.

Matthew 3.13—17

57

You cannot ignore this canvas in the biblical art gallery. All four evangelists (a rare combination) see to that; and one of them, St Luke, even gives it an elaborate date. So you cannot dismiss it as barren of historical content even if you recognize, as you must, the symbolic elements in the composition — the descending dove and the voice from heaven. Something tremendous is happening here.

First of all we see Jesus striding in from Nazareth where he had shut his carpenter's shop door for the last time and said farewell to his family. He was leaving his private life for ever; in future he would be up on the public stage with little relief from the pressure of constant ministry. So this approach to John baptizing in the River Jordan was the great turning point in his life. There could be no going back.

Now we see John. Did he sense all the implications of Jesus' crisis time? Or was he merely overcome by the incongruity of Jesus trekking down to the river for cleansing and repentance, amongst the shuffling crowd around him? The fourth gospel would have us understand that he had been inwardly alerted to the revelation that would come to him about the one on whom he would see the Holy Spirit descending. Small wonder, then, that he held back at Jesus' approach. The turning point of his, John's, life too had come; from now on he would decrease but Jesus would increase. History was being made at the River Jordan that day. History with world consequences. History with eternal consequences. God's plan 'to fulfil all righteousness' was to be carried out.

John protested — he could not baptize Jesus. But Jesus insisted and went down into the water as if he were a common penitent. He was not a common penitent, though; not a penitent at all. He was declared to be at that moment what he already was, God's 'beloved Son' with whom God was 'well pleased', and as such there and then he was anointed for his ministry with the Holy Spirit, God's creative and redeeming spirit, the spirit of power. Did the surrounding crowd know? There was no thunderclap, no shaking of the earth's foundation; the equipping of Jesus was so silent, so gentle, that it could only be likened to the descent of a dove. But John knew. And Jesus knew, for he was granted God's voice of assurance as to his identity and ministry. No longer was he the carpenter of Nazareth, but the man of the divine spirit with a task to perform.

★　★　★

Jesus had seen that mixed multitude lining up for baptism. He had not only seen them, he had mingled with them, he had stood with them in the queue waiting to be baptized, he had heard their conversation, he had looked into their eyes — shifty eyes some of them, and eyes full of pain, angry eyes, rebellious eyes, sad eyes, compassionate eyes, and some in the queue with sightless eyes, led by relatives or friends. They were all there, shuffling along, old men and women, bent almost double, and here and there protesting; proud and pompous individuals holding their noses because of the smell — body smell and the smell of dirty clothing. All these were to constitute the sphere of Jesus' ministry: he wished to be identified with them. This is why he stood in the queue. This is why he went down into the water to be baptized, not because he was a penitent. The Holy Spirit had identified him with these (for the most part) 'dirty' people. And there you have the gospel, the good news of his baptism, the message this picture has been painted to portray — God with us all, in the midst of our broken and imperfect humanity.

Prayer

> Lord, let me be open to people
> > as you were open to people,
> > attractive people,
> > unattractive people.
> Lord, let me be a compassionate Christian,
> > not a weak sentimental Christian
> > but wise, far-seeing and spiritually-minded,
> > caring for people's deepest as well as for
> > > their immediate needs.
> Lord, equip me by your Holy Spirit.

Carried to healing

2 And when he returned to Capernaum after some days, it was reported that he was at home. ²And many were gathered together, so

that there was no longer room for them, not even about the door; and he was preaching the word to them. ³And they came, bringing to him a paralytic carried by four men. ⁴And when they could not get near him because of the crowd, they removed the roof above him; and when they had made an opening, they let down the pallet on which the paralytic lay. ⁵And when Jesus saw their faith, he said to the paralytic, 'My son, your sins are forgiven'. ⁶Now some of the scribes were sitting there, questioning in their hearts, ⁷'Why does this man speak thus? It is blasphemy! Who can forgive sins but God alone?' ⁸And immediately Jesus, perceiving in his spirit that they thus questioned within themselves, said to them, 'Why do you question thus in your hearts? ⁹Which is easier, to say to the paralytic, "Your sins are forgiven", or to say, "Rise, take up your pallet and walk"? ¹⁰But that you may know that the Son of man has authority on earth to forgive sins' — he said to the paralytic — ¹¹'I say to you, rise, take up your pallet and go home'. ¹²And he rose, and immediately took up the pallet and went out before them all; so that they were all amazed and glorified God, saying, 'We never saw anything like this!'

Mark 2.1—12 (RSV)

Everywhere in Capernaum the excited news spread: 'He's back! He's at home!' Ever since that memorable evening after sunset, when the whole town, carrying their sick, crowded round the door of Peter's house because Jesus had dramatically cured his fever-stricken mother-in-law (Mark 1.29—34), they had missed him. He had been absent on a tour of the local countryside preaching in the synagogues and healing both the mentally and physically ill. It had been a whirlwind of activity, reaching a climax when by the touch of his hand he had risked contagion to cleanse a leper. After that no synagogue was sufficiently large to accommodate the crowds: people streamed in from all quarters, so much so that he was forced to avoid the towns and villages and to conduct his ministry in the open country.

And now he was back in Capernaum in Simon Peter's house where he was staying. At once the crowds built up. All round the door in the street they stood waiting to catch a glimpse of him and listening intently to his charismatic teaching. And when a little group of lawyers arrived, operators of the civil and religious law, they made way for them. So they, too, sat there watching and listening. All were too engrossed to be aware of the commotion outside caused by four men carrying a paralyzed man on a mattress, jostling the reluctant bystanders to make a passage for them through to the house. But they had no chance: the crowd was thick, and unrelenting. But they would not be defeated: they were determined to take their victim of acute paralysis to Jesus for healing. There was nothing for it but to climb to the roof by means of the outside stairway, break it open and let down their patient into the room. The operation was not difficult: the roofs of many Palestinian houses were constructed of beams and rafters over which were spread branches of trees and twigs, the whole made firm with earth trodden hard and baked by the sun. What did it matter if the listening people below were spattered with dust and rubble! Their purpose would be achieved. And it was. Jesus looked up to see four brown faces peering over the edge of a large hole and a mattress being gently lowered on which lay a frightened paralyzed man.

We can well imagine Jesus smiling as he watched this novel approach of a patient for healing. It is hard to see him as the intensely human person he was if he did not. Not that Peter would be smiling — he would have to mend the hole in the roof! But there are other dimensions to this incident. First the sufferer on the mattress needed reassurance, and Jesus gave it. '*Teknon*' is the word; in Greek it is almost a term of endearment — 'My dear young fellow!' And then this surprising statement: 'Your sins are forgiven'. Did Jesus see with that extraordinary insight of his that the root of this man's malady was not physical but some kind of spiritual atrophy? Not that he believed that all illness is the result of sin, but there is a connection between mind and body; a serious defect in the one can be the cause of serious defect in the other as psychiatrists and holistic health practitioners will tell us today. And so to the rigid man on the mattress Jesus spoke the releasing words strong and clear, 'your sins are forgiven', for faith was obvious, faith in his power to heal, faith on the part of the four bearers, faith perhaps also on the part of the one borne.

But were they not only surprised but disappointed? Restoration of lost physical powers was what they were seeking, not a religious pronouncement. And what of the lawyers watching, critically assessing the situation? Were their suspicions aroused — suspicions of blasphemy, the penalty for which was stoning? Did they now possess evidence to report to the authorities? Was a case against Jesus building up? 'Who but God can forgive sins?' they thought to themselves. Jesus read them as they sat there. 'Why do you harbour thoughts like these? Is it easier to say to the paralyzed man, "Your sins are forgiven" or to say, "Stand up, take your bed, and walk"?' They recognized the logic. They could scarcely miss it. The pronunciation of forgiveness, being incapable of proof, is easier than telling a crippled man to walk. The latter could be seen, and seeing is believing. So Jesus proceeded to operate in the *apparently* more difficult area — physical healing — to demonstrate his power in the spiritual. He went on, 'But to convince you that the Son of man has the right on earth to forgive sins' — he turned to the paralyzed man — 'I say to you, stand up, take your bed, and go home'. No statement this time but a command, because the man's co-operation in his physical healing was necessary. And he gave it, looking at Jesus and hearing his word gave him the will. He got up, lifted up his mattress and with it went out before the crowds at the door. They made a gangway, for astonishment, if not awe, had seized them all.

★   ★   ★

As we stand back to contemplate this extraordinary scene what do we see? Primarily, it speaks of the interdependence of human beings upon one another and is a moving reminder of that basic human kindness that has never been wholly lost in any place at any time. Four men so concerned about a fifth, a neighbour, and his crippling incapacity that they were willing to carry him, bed and all, along the street for healing, and if need be break up someone's roof to accomplish their mission of mercy. We ought never wholly to lose faith in human nature.

We also see a stronger faith, reinforcing the goodness that already exists; faith in the power of this divine healer called Jesus. And see too, this unconventional declaration of the forgiveness of sins in that it follows on no expression of repentance, indeed no one speaks at all except Jesus. All the emphasis falls on action which implied faith — four men willing to go to unusual lengths somehow to get to Jesus. And had the paralytic himself faith in that he was willing to be carried up those back steps and be lowered through the roof? Could it be that repentance sometimes follows faith instead of preceding it, repentance that is as a sense of unworthiness for the gift of healing faith has attracted?

Perhaps we are left with a mood of self-examination in the presence of this picture. How often have we been prepared to act as a porter in carrying some needy neighbour in prayer to God who alone can heal in depth? And what of our persistence? How good are we at accepting other people's help ourselves? The picture probes us.

Prayer

> Lord, thank you for the praying church
> for praying friends
> for praying people who care.
> At times I have been brought down too low to pray.
> Prayers 'won't come',
> prayers seem pointless.
> But others have carried me by their prayers
> into your presence,
> your compassionate presence,
> your healing presence.
> They have made a hole for me in the roof
> and I have 'come through'.
> Blessed be your holy name.

Limited ministries

[21]And Jesus went away from there and withdrew to the district of Tyre and Sidon. [22]And behold, a Canaanite woman from that region came out and cried, 'Have mercy on me, O Lord, Son of David; my daughter is severely possessed by a demon'. [23]But he did not answer her a word. And his disciples came and begged him, saying, 'Send her away, for she is crying after us'. [24]He answered, 'I was sent only to the lost sheep of the house of Israel'. [25]But she came and knelt before him, saying, 'Lord, help me'. [26]And he answered, 'It is not fair to take the children's bread and throw it to the dogs'. [27]She said, 'Yes, Lord, yet even the dogs eat the crumbs that fall from their masters' table'. [28]Then

Jesus answered her, 'O woman, great is your faith! Be it done for you as you desire'. And her daughter was healed instantly.

Matthew 15.21—28 (RSV)

Not all the canvasses in a great art gallery are massive, some are diminutive; and though exhibited, for they merit exhibition, nevertheless are tucked away in a corner where probably only the knowledgeable take the trouble to find them. Such a picture in the New Testament is that of the Greek woman desperate to make contact with Jesus.

The woman captures our attention first of all; clearly a foreigner, most likely pagan, she is intelligent but driven to desperation by the fury of the psychic disturbance that had afflicted her daughter and over whom her mother-heart was bleeding. She must find relief, any relief, anywhere. Then the unbelievable news reached her ears: the Jewish healer, Jesus, of whom everyone was speaking was near, actually on the Tyrian border, close to, if not actually in, Gentile territory where she lived. This was her chance. But to her despair she could not find him. Her only success was meeting his disciples. So she pestered them making herself a nuisance like some persistent beggar whom they unsuccessfully attempted to shake off.

Meanwhile Jesus was in hiding, not consciously from this woman but, as it were, in retreat. All but worn out with a dawn-to-dusk ministry, and forever facing growing opposition which sooner or later must come to a head, he had sought peace no doubt to pray and to think. Every leader from time to time must seek such occasions of renewal. Jesus had even freed himself from his disciples' company.

Then this woman appeared. She had tracked him down. 'Sir! Have pity on me, Son of David, my daughter is tormented by a devil'. But for all the compassion in Jesus' eyes as he looked into that eager yet strained foreign face he uttered not a single word. Her plea was met with silence. Then the disciples came on the scene giving voice to their exasperation at the effrontery of this woman's intrusion. 'Send her away' they called to Jesus, 'see how she comes shouting after us'. He did not send her away but a sigh might well have escaped his lips: all around him in this Gentile territory were heaps of crying human need of which this woman's was typical. He agonized to meet it. But what could he do? What ought he to do? He knew without a shadow of doubt that his was a divinely appointed ministry to one people only, strictly limited. His troubled thoughts actually broke into words, 'I was sent only to the lost sheep of the house of Israel'.

But this woman before him was now on her knees at his feet pathetically appealing, 'Help me, Sir'. Still the limitation of his ministry held him back — 'It is not fair to take the children's bread and throw it to the dogs'. Was he still speaking to himself perhaps? To our ears, in any case, it sounds harsh in the extreme; but not to this woman's ears. She caught hopefully at the word she noticed Jesus had used for 'dogs' — not the street dogs which roamed most Eastern towns, filthy, fierce scavengers, the kind the Jews had in mind when they spurned Gentiles as dogs, but 'little dogs', *kunaria* in Greek, of which the Greeks made pets in their homes. Now this woman was most likely a Greek. Quick to spot the word he used she replied, 'Yes, Lord, yet the little dogs eat the crumbs that fall from their masters' table'. They are *not* banished. They are *not* starved. Their needs *are met*. Who can doubt that at that moment the strain had lifted from her eyes? Hope was shining there instead. She knew Jesus had the power to heal her daughter and now she saw he would exercise it for her. He responded to that faith, 'O woman, great is your faith. Be it done for you as you desire.' And when she reached home she saw how her faith was justified.

★　★　★

When we walk away from the picture gallery we cannot help thinking of this little painting. It is a touching and thought-provoking scene. Do we rebel against the thought of Jesus' limited ministry? All ministries, though, are limited and we only succeed in them if we accept their limitation. Every man, every woman, must discover what is his or her gift and work at that in the place where he or she has been set down. There may certainly be occasions when to break out of the limitation may be right, especially to meet human need, but they should be exceptional: the principle of love rather than any other rigid principle should dictate the rules. Jesus was constrained by race, culture and history, but, through obedience to his limited calling, he opened the means of salvation to all humanity. Like Jesus, we must not be ashamed to share and respect human limitation.

Prayer

Lord, sometimes I kick out at the limitations of my life.
    My scene of operation seems so small,
        so limited,
        so unglamorous.
    I am tempted to think I could accomplish
        so much more somewhere else.
Help me, Lord, to be faithful to what you have given me to do.

The disturbing guest

---

[36]One of the Pharisees asked him to eat with him, and he went into the Pharisee's house, and took his place at table. [37]And behold, a woman of the city, who was a sinner, when she learned that he was at table in the Pharisee's house, brought an alabaster flask of ointment, [38]and standing behind him at his feet, weeping, she began to wet his feet with her tears, and wiped them with the hair of her head, and kissed his feet, and anointed them with the ointment. [39]Now when the Pharisee who had invited him saw it, he said to himself, 'If this man were a prophet, he would have known who and what sort of woman this is who is touching him, for she is a sinner'. [40]And Jesus answering said to him, 'Simon, I have something to say to you'. And he answered, 'What is it, Teacher?' [41]'A certain creditor had two debtors; one owed five hundred denarii, and the other fifty. [42]When they could not pay, he forgave them both. Now which of them will love him more?' [43]Simon answered, 'The one, I suppose, to whom he forgave more'. And he said to him, 'You have judged rightly'. [44]Then turning toward the woman he said to Simon, 'Do you see this woman? I entered your house, you gave me no water for my feet, but she has wet my feet with her tears and wiped them with her hair. [45]You gave me no kiss, but from the time I came in she has not ceased to kiss my feet. [46]You did not anoint my head with oil, but she has anointed my feet with ointment. [47]Therefore I tell you, her sins, which are many, are forgiven, for

she loved much; but he who is forgiven little, loves little'. [48]And he said to her, 'Your sins are forgiven'. [49]Then those who were at table with him began to say among themselves, 'Who is this, who even forgives sins?' [50]And he said to the woman, 'Your faith has saved you; go in peace'.

Luke 7.36—50 (RSV)

Before us is a dinner table ready set; couches drawn up for the guests; servants waiting. Simon, the host, a strictly religious man, is proud to use his house for social entertaining. Many interesting people have been met through his invitations. But who is this crossing the threshold? Jesus of Nazareth? Does he attend social functions? Apparently, and not infrequently. But Simon the host does not greet him with the common courtesies, nor are the servants at the door permitted to perform for him the customary washing of the guests' dusty feet. It would be interesting now to watch the reactions of this itinerant preacher when confronted with 'polite society'; his lowly origin and status might not be blurred. Ungreeted and tacitly disrespected, Jesus found his place at table.

Then the worst happened. A woman appeared, but not just a woman — women were ostracized anyway in that society — but a prostitute known and recognized. She had entered secretly (not that this was difficult in the open-planning of an eastern household) and took up a position behind Jesus, close to his feet. All eyes were turned on her though not Jesus': he was looking at Simon, his acutely embarrassed host.

And there was more to come, indeed, a vulgar emotional exhibition ensued. The woman wept. Her uncontrolled tears wetted Jesus' unwashed feet; she then proceeded to wipe them with her long loose hair which only unrespectable women let loose in public. Having let loose her unrestrained love, regardless of the other guests contemptuously watching, she actually kissed his feet. Then, revealing that the encounter was by her own design she uncorked the tiny flask carrying the myrrh she had brought especially to anoint the feet of the man she adored. To the Pharisees and others reclining at table the scene was thoroughly offensive.

Jesus kept his eye on Simon, his condescending host. He could see what he was thinking. 'If this man were a real prophet, he would have known who and what sort of woman this is who is

67

touching him, for she is a sinner'. 'Simon' he said, 'I have something to say to you.' 'What is it, Teacher?' he countered with a politeness befitting his status. The parable Jesus told in reply was so neat it must have been the shortest he ever told: 'A certain creditor had two debtors; one owed him five hundred denarii, and the other fifty. When they could not pay, he forgave them both'. Then Jesus asked Simon, 'Now which of them will love him more?'

The guests waited. Jesus, the slighted one, had become the centre of attention. Far from being outclassed by the kind of clever conversation they catered for in the parties they arranged, he was actually leading it. Eyes were transferred from Jesus to Simon. His reply dragged itself out, 'The one I suppose, to whom he forgave more'. 'You have judged rightly', said Jesus, reducing the Pharisee to the dimension of a schoolboy in one of his classes satisfying his teacher with a correct answer. Ten out of ten! Then Jesus went on to give a direct comparison between Simon and the woman: 'you gave me no water for my feet, but she has wet my feet with her tears . . . You gave me no kiss, but . . . she has not ceased to kiss my feet. You did not anoint my head with oil, but she has anointed my feet with ointment'. So the woman's many sins were forgiven 'for she loved much', but 'he who is forgiven little, loves little'. This woman, rejected and despised by conventional society, had been accepted and forgiven, in spite of her past and her immense sin. The outpouring of her love had cleansed her body and soul.

The artist does not reveal how this party broke up. We are only told that a disturbing question began to haunt the minds of the guests — the identity of Jesus. 'Who is this, who even forgives sins?' Who indeed? Did the woman know? Well might we ask as we imagine her hurrying from the scene her face transformed and with Jesus' words ringing in her ears, 'Your faith has saved you; go in peace'.

★　　★　　★

This picture conjures up so many familiar prejudices, fears, judgmental posturings. We are so often blinded and restrained by accepted values that we seldom stop to reassess our own priorities being only too ready to condemn those who are disadvantaged or 'disreputable' in some way. If we pause and imagine Jesus sitting among us as a guest, he may well catch us on the wrong foot as he did with Simon the Pharisee and expose our failings. We cannot put Jesus where we want him for, before we know where we are, he is putting us where he wants us to be. Entertaining Jesus is not an easy option and his forgiveness is never cheap. We shall probably be greatly discomforted by Jesus before we experience his peace.

Prayer

> Lord, save me from being a hypocrite.
> When I look around and see those who have
>   made a mess of their lives,
>   some through their own fault,
>   most through the fault of circumstance
>   or the fault of others,
>   I am tempted to look down on them,
>   forgetting my own sins.
>
> The Pharisees were well meaning.
> But they slipped as I, too, easily slip
>   into spiritual pride,
>   pride of achievement,
>   pride of status.
> Lord, forgive me for being half a hypocrite,
>   maybe more than half.
> I am a sinner;
> I need your forgiveness.

So little — so much

[9]'There is a lad here who has five barley loaves and two fish; but what are they among so many?' [10]Jesus said, 'Make the people sit down'. Now there was much grass in the place; so the men sat down, in number about five thousand. [11]Jesus then took the loaves, and when he had given thanks, he distributed them to those who were seated; so also the fish, as much as they wanted.

John 6.9–11 (RSV)

69

Observe first the boy with his five barley loaves and two fish, little fish no doubt — the Greek word *opsaria* is used — to be eaten as a kind of relish to compensate for the dryness of the bread. Perhaps his mother sent him out for the day with this picnic and he had wandered along until he joined up with crowds of people all moving in one direction, soon to find himself listening to a man preaching. Everyone seemed spellbound and they were still sitting there hours later. But the boy did not move; and he had not eaten his picnic — he did not like to because no one around him had any food for themselves.

Then a man asked him for his picnic, all five loaves and the two fish, and ushered him up to the preacher. He did not know what to say. Imagine the picture: this huge crowd, desperately hungry, and there in front of it this boy thrust forward with five barley loaves and two little fish, as if such a meagre amount could provide for so many. Could any situation be more absurd? The boy, perhaps reluctantly, surrendered his picnic. Jesus took it, gave thanks as if this were a public banquet and distributed it to the famished crowds. All had sufficient.

The German New Testament in Modern Speech has a line drawing of the boy inserted in the text with this caption:

So wenig was du zu bieten hast —
So viel, wenn Christus es weitergibt.

So little you have to offer —
So much, when Christ gives it away.

How are we to interpret this episode? Do we walk away from the picture feeling that it bears no resemblance to reality and has little to say to us? Or perhaps we seek a rationalistic explanation to make it more credible. Perhaps many people in the crowd *did* have food with them but held on to it secretly, not wanting to share it with those who had none. On seeing the boy surrender his picnic, people followed his example. The 'miracle' was people made willing to share their possessions — a rarity, but possible in Christ's presence. 'Let everyone share what he has and there will be enough for all.'

Such an interpretation is appealing in many ways but it enables us to see only half the picture. Is a spontaneous outburst of public generosity the message which this picture has been painted to convey or is there not a deeper way of looking at it, a way which incorporates the divine action as well as the human response? After all, it was Jesus' action, we are told, that fired the enthusiasm of the crowd, not the boy's. Notice the place of this picture in the art gallery: in St John's gospel, it is followed by Jesus' sermon on the Bread of Life, namely Christ himself. It looks as if the purpose of the feeding of the five thousand was not to inspire the relief of physical hunger, right and proper as this ministry is, but rather it was performed as a sign of the real presence of God in both power and compassion. It is this mystery which draws Christians to the Eucharist when the bread and wine are offered to God, distributed, and shared by us.

★   ★   ★

Deep and weighty questions are raised by this scene which we dare not dodge. But come back to the boy. Come back to something simple.

> So little you have to offer —
> So much, when Christ gives it away.

Have you said to yourself, 'How little I have to offer to forward the Christian gospel and way of life in a world that seems to have lost its direction in a bog of materialism. I can't preach sermons. I can't be an itinerant evangelist. I can't organize a spiritual revival in the land'? But we can begin with a little and accomplish a great deal if we are prepared to surrender something of our time and talents. If you are a churchgoer you could refrain from being evasive about it among your friends and work associates and follow a lifestyle that bears the mark of your Christian allegiance. Not much maybe, but it takes courage when in Rome *not* to do as Rome does for Christ's sake. Only a little, but the boy in the picture before us gave his little for Christ to use and *he made it much*. And note this: many benefitted in consequence. They benefitted because of the power of Christ, but this operated because of what the boy gave up. Don't forget the boy.

Prayer

> Lord, I cannot claim to possess an intellectual faith.
> > I would shrink from an examination
> > even on the contents of the Bible.
> > But I believe in you,

> I trust you,
> I have committed my life to you.
> If I am pressed today to disclose my faith,
>   simple as it is,
>   let me not hold back.
>   You multiply what we offer
>   for the good of others.

A glimpse of glory

²And after six days Jesus took with him Peter and James and John, and led them up a high mountain apart by themselves; and he was transfigured before them, ³and his garments became glistening, intensely white, as no fuller on earth could bleach them . . . ⁷And a cloud overshadowed them, and a voice came out of the cloud, 'This is my beloved Son; listen to him'.

Mark 9.2–3, 7 (RSV)

If you asked for five pictures covering the most important events in the life of Jesus, the transfiguration would have to be one of them. The other four would be his birth, baptism, death and resurrection. But who knows about the transfiguration? What does the word mean anyway? We don't hear it in the supermarket, nor are we likely to overhear someone talking about transfiguration in the bus queue as they may about Christmas, Good Friday, or Easter. So what happened? And what has it to do with us?

Look into the background: Jesus was under pressure, terrible pressure. His enemies were closing in and he knew it. He may not have ever seen the victim of a crucifixion, but they were not that rare. The Romans used crucifixion as a deterrent against rebellion and so the crucified victims were left on show by roadsides. Jesus was now listed by the authorities as a rebel and unless he altered his message drastically, capitulated or escaped across the frontier, crucifixion was what loomed up for him at the end of the road. But he could not talk about it even to his disciples, who would not understand; they thought in terms of a messianic political triumph not a sacrificial death. So Jesus was horribly alone.

So, taking three of his closest disciples, Jesus climbed a nearby mountain to lay the whole frightful dilemma before God in prayer. And there in the loneliness and before the eyes of these three men he was transformed or transfigured. They were astonished, even afraid. They scarcely recognized him: the ordinary Galilean man they knew so well shone like some celestial figure. And then, from the cloud shrouding the whole vision, came a voice proclaiming 'This is my beloved Son; listen to him'.

What do we have before us then — a fairy tale scene in a land of makebelieve? Far from it. I will tell you what I see in this picture.

What I see first of all in the transfiguration story is no doubt extremely simple: I see an example of God's infinite mercy in encouraging Jesus, his faithful servant, in the awesome ministry that faced him in the very near future, absolutely alone. Maybe you think Jesus did not need encouragement. But he was a human being like you and me set in a world that can sometimes turn nasty. Most of us know how this feels. Consider someone who has lost their job; a single parent struggling to bring up a child; an employee whose employer has turned against him; teenagers who have failed their examinations. And suppose they are alone with no one to share their fear. Fortunate is the person who at such times believes in a God who provides for us in unexpected ways an encouraging experience when we are down in the drains of apprehension. God sustains his servants who trust him. God knows and God cares. This is the message I see first of all in this transfiguration scene.

And now I see something else. We need experiences of awe, wonder and grandeur in our lives. If we believe the gospel we must believe that at the end of our earthly pilgrimage is glory. So we need, from time to time, anticipations of that glory: we cannot continue with a perpetual round of ordinariness.

I remember some years ago sitting on the deck of a boat on Lake Thun in Switzerland travelling from Interlaken to Spiez. All the passengers, including myself, sitting side by side were rather glum: we were hoping for a beautiful evening, so that we could revel in the panoramic beauty all round us, but instead, nothing but murky cloud wrapped up everything in a depressing greyness. All of a sudden a Frenchman jumped up and pointing with arms out-stretched cried out, at the top of his voice, 'Regardez, regardez'. And we did; dozens and dozens of us looked to where he was pointing. There in a sudden break in the clouds was the complete Jungfrau, its snowcap gleaming with a dazzling whiteness tinged with pink evening sunlight, all against a background of azure sky. It was a transfiguration and it took our breath away. Our boat chugged on and the murky mist clamped down on us, but we had had our vision of glory and spent the rest of the journey contented.

Let the transfiguration scene, then, remind us that around us are wonders to part the clouds of life a little so that we may catch a glimpse of the eternal glory, providing us with another dimension to life's plainness and sometimes drabness. We are destined for eternity and God has not forgotten us.

★　　★　　★

Jesus was transfigured on that mountain top in Galilee and after-wards the three disciples saw him differently. He was in their eyes no longer simply the superb teacher, the astonishing healer and the strong leader of twelve assorted men. He was the Son of God beyond compare, an awesome figure. None of us has seen Jesus properly — until we have glimpsed this other dimension. He it is before whom, at the end of the day, we can but bow our heads and worship, 'My Lord and my God'. Jesus needs to be transfigured for us, changed from being only an impressive figure in history into a divine presence we can trust, the risen Christ. Church worship is one area which can provide us with a flash of eternal glory. In scrip-ture and sacrament is presented the light which shines, sometimes hazily, sometimes dazzlingly, leading us to the transfigured Christ and his transforming power.

Prayer

> Lord, all my days seem the same.
>> I know exactly when I shall get up.
>> I know exactly when I shall go to bed.
>> And there is the same train to catch,
>> the same office desk at which to sit,

the same faces to encounter in the
        supermarket check-out.
This is my world. I know it backwards. I know it forwards.
Forgive me, Lord, if sometimes I cry out at this sameness.
    Be merciful and let me see some glory;
    I need lifting up.
    'Thou art the King of Glory, O Christ.'
    Show me your glory.

The donkey ride

---

[12]The next day a great crowd who had come to the feast heard that Jesus was coming to Jerusalem. [13]So they took branches of palm trees and went out to meet him, crying, 'Hosanna! Blessed is he who comes in the name of the Lord, even the King of Israel!' [14]And Jesus found a young ass and sat upon it; as it is written,

[15]'Fear not, daughter of Zion;
behold, your king is coming,
sitting on an ass's colt!'

John 12.12—15 (RSV)

Picture Jesus' feet touching the ground: they must have done because this account in St John's gospel tells us he found a little donkey and sat on it. He needed no 'leg up' into the stirrups — there weren't any. In our churches on Palm Sunday we hear about Christ's *triumphal* entry into Jerusalem, but no one could possibly pose as triumphant on a little donkey with feet touching the ground, or for that matter on a full-grown donkey. Even though the donkey has been for centuries an indispensable animal in the Middle East, no one could label a donkey an impressive creature; indeed, it is somewhat comic either when braying or stubbornly silent.

Nevertheless crowds of people clustered close to Jesus on his donkey ride into Jerusalem, both city dwellers and pilgrims up from the country for the Passover festival. People love processions. But do not miss those Roman faces in the background: the military kept a low profile during Passover week but watched every movement in the crowds, ready to pounce on any incipient riot. They watched Jesus on his little donkey. How jeeringly they must have laughed over what they saw! Perhaps some had witnessed a triumphal procession in the forum in Rome at the conclusion of a military conquest. What splendour and power! What humiliation for the prisoners of war dragged in chains behind their captors, some of them of noble blood. And here in contrast this pathetic procession into Jerusalem, the central figure on a little donkey his feet touching the ground! And the cheering crowds having no flags or banners were driven to cut down branches of palm trees and wave them to accompany their shouting. What comic stories the Roman soldiers must have told to one another that night.

Why did Jesus allow this procession? It seems out of character. Throughout his ministry he studiously avoided publicity, so much so that he had been called 'the secret messiah'. 'Do not tell anyone' was a typical command to people he had healed, so why the donkey ride now? We all know that people love processions, banner waving and cheering. And this day was part of their holiday festival, the Passover. They were bursting to pour forth their pilgrim psalms of praise. And there, marching with them to Jerusalem was this Jesus whose fame in word and deed had spread throughout the land. They simply had to shout hosannas, making him their centre-piece. Their enthusiasm was unstoppable. And Jesus let them have it. He did not want to spoil their fun.

But look a little closer. The procession came to nothing. There was no confrontation with the authorities, no powers were toppled, no organization of people's power, no demands. On reaching the Temple Jesus looked round and went home. The day fizzled out. Palm Sunday on any common reckoning was an anti-climax.

★   ★   ★

It is within the apparent absurdity and anti-climax of this whole scene that the meaning of this event and the message about Jesus are to be discerned. The way of working of God's servant is not via the pressure of crowds, trumped-up excitement, or indeed of anything whatsoever that is overpowering. It is the complete antithesis. He comes on a little donkey with his feet touching the ground. He approaches people humbly so that they can respond freely to the mystery of his loving forgiveness: he does not challenge them with an aggressive or spectacular show of what he can do. In this way, his full redemptive power is realized. Time and again in the gospels we learn how people are saved through their recognition of who Jesus was and faith in his goodness. Spiritual discernment, not flag waving or superficial shouting, is required to discern the identity of Jesus and the purpose of his mission. He rode to Jerusalem on Palm Sunday on a little donkey with his feet touching the ground, and allowed the whole popularly organized demonstration to peter out. The message of Palm Sunday is there, just there. So John capped it with his abbreviated caption from Zechariah 9.9:

> Fear not, daughter of Zion;
> behold, your king is coming,
> sitting on an ass's colt.

And within the week Jesus was in another procession, this time heading for Calvary and behind him a press-ganged man from the country carrying his instrument of execution, a heavy wooden cross.

Prayer

> Lord, when I see you on your little donkey,
>   I don't know whether to laugh or cry.
>   I can't laugh, because it seems so out of place,
>   and I can't cry because it seems
>   such useless sentiment.
>   I ought, I suppose, to shout
>   'Hosanna,
>   Blessed is He that cometh in the name of the Lord',
>   and I will, for I see this donkey ride
>   from the other side of Easter.
> You rode that little creature to show
>   what kind of king you are,
>   never forcing,
>   never overpowering,
>   never threatening.

But you approach us even now
    in the humblest of ways
    so that we may receive you
    as you truly are
    our living Lord and Saviour.

The last supper

¹⁰Then Judas Iscariot, who was one of the twelve, went to the chief priests in order to betray him to them. ¹¹And when they heard it they were glad, and promised to give him money. And he sought an opportunity to betray him.

¹²And on the first day of Unleavened Bread, when they sacrificed the passover lamb, his disciples said to him, 'Where will you have us go and prepare for you to eat the passover?' ¹³And he sent two of his disciples, and said to them, 'Go into the city, and a man carrying a jar of water will meet you; follow him, ¹⁴and wherever he enters, say to the householder, "The Teacher says, Where is my guest room, where I am to eat the passover with my disciples?" ¹⁵And he will show you a large upper room furnished and ready; there prepare for us'. ¹⁶And the disciples set out and went to the city, and found it as he had told them; and they prepared the passover.

¹⁷And when it was evening he came with the twelve. ¹⁸And as they were at table eating, Jesus said, 'Truly, I say to you, one of you will betray me, one who is eating with me'. ¹⁹They began to be sorrowful, and to say to him one after another, 'Is it I?' ²⁰He said to them, 'It is one of the twelve, one who is dipping bread into the dish with me. ²¹For the Son of man goes as it is written of him, but woe to that man by whom the Son of man is betrayed! It would have been better for that man if he had not been born'.

²²And as they were eating, he took bread, and blessed, and broke it, and gave it to them, and said, 'Take; this is my body'. ²³And he took a cup, and when he had given thanks he gave it to them, and they all drank of it. ²⁴And he said to them, 'This is my blood of the covenant, which is poured out for many. ²⁵Truly, I say to you, I shall not drink

again of the fruit of the vine until that day when I drink it new in the kingdom of God'.

[26]And when they had sung a hymn, they went out to the Mount of Olives.

Mark 14.10—26 (RSV)

When we look closely at what has come to be called the last supper we notice how secret it all was. It had to be. The priests in Jerusalem were desperate: they were bent on doing away with Jesus, and they knew that he was at hand in the city, but hidden among the crowds of pilgrims gathered for the Passover feast, thousands of them. How could they arrest him? Not openly — that would result in a riot. Their only hope lay in the possibility of a defection among his twelve disciples. So when Judas Iscariot secretly presented himself before them they seized their chance. Money passed hands, Temple money, and Judas crept back to rejoin the disciples. Did any of them query his absence from among them? He could have been making purchases for their Passover; after all he kept the purse.

Meanwhile Jesus, too, had been secretly active. He had made contact with a householder in Jerusalem who was a secret sympathizer in order to arrange a room where he could eat the Passover meal with his disciples. But no one must know, not even the twelve disciples and certainly not Judas. So the plan was to post a man-servant in the street carrying a jar of water who would be told how two men would contact him there. No words were to be spoken; he was to allow them to follow him back to the house where inside they would give the password to the householder, 'The Teacher says, Where is my guest room (*katalyma*) where I may eat the passover with my disciples?' All worked according to plan; the two disciples made that secret contact with the householder, but they had had one surprise: they were not shown the *katalyma* or ground-floor meeting place where other pilgrims might gather, (for every available space in Jerusalem was let at the time of the Passover) but, instead, a large upper room, furnished. They went up to it, no doubt by an outside stairway, noting how secret it was. There was only one entrance. No stranger could pass through.

In the evening, when the city street was all but deserted, Jesus and the twelve disciples, including Judas, ascended to that upper room, where the meal was set out and the couches around the table had been arranged by the two disciples. No servants were present.

79

It was Jesus' last supper; it was secret and exclusive. When the meal began, Jesus announced that one of the twelve would betray him and was met with disbelief. When all professed ignorance of who it could possibly be Jesus said, 'It is one of the twelve, one who is dipping bread into the dish with me'. Was it then that Judas left the table, hurried down the stairway, out into the night, to inform the priests where Jesus might be found? Did the other disciples query the sudden departure of Judas? Or did they think that Jesus had tacitly asked him to slip out to purchase extra provisions, or perhaps make a donation to some poverty-stricken people outside? Who knows what they thought?

The Passover meal meanwhile was overshadowed by Jesus' intimation that this was to be his last meal with them. Then he took bread, and blessed and broke it — they had seen him do this a hundred times with those strong, work-worn carpenter's hands of his — and gave it to them, now with the awesome words 'This is my body'. Likewise, with the cup full of red wine, 'This is my blood of the covenant, which is poured out for many'. They all shared the bread and drank some of the wine. Jesus talked for a while deeply and calmly. Then they sang a hymn, possibly from what is called the *Hallel*, Psalms 115—118, and trooped out to the Mount of Olives not far away. They would have been in time not to be caught in the room by Judas and his nefarious accomplices.

★   ★   ★

As we stand gazing at this famous picture we think of how the last supper has become the Lord's Supper, the Holy Communion, the Eucharist, or the Mass in the life of the Christian Church down the centuries, and of the battles, not only of words sad to say, that have accompanied its interpretation. It cannot have survived merely as a memorial of an historical event. In our worship it must minister to the partakers of it now. Bread is the staff of life, wine is the living substance of life. It is Christ's bread, and Christ's wine that is given to us in this act of worship. In the original historical event it was associated as closely as it could be with the sacrifice of his body and blood on the cross; the one followed the other within a matter of hours. He gave himself for us there, and gives himself to us now. If any place exists where a casual attitude is wholly inappropriate surely it is here. The last supper was not casual: it was carefully planned and safeguarded, secret, and exclusive. And it was more: a solemn occasion carried out against a background of betrayal.

Prayer

> Bread of heaven, on thee we feed,
> For thy Flesh is meat indeed;
> Ever may our souls be fed
> With this true and living Bread;
> Day by day with strength supplied
> Through the life of him who died.

J. Conder

The paradox of Christ's powerlessness

[38]Then two robbers were crucified with him, one on the right and one on the left. [39]And those who passed by derided him, wagging their heads [40]and saying, 'You who would destroy the temple and build it in three days, save yourself! If you are the Son of God, come down from the cross'. [41]So also the chief priests, with the scribes and elders, mocked him, saying, [42]'He saved others' he cannot save himself. He is the King of Israel; let him come down now from the cross, and we will believe in him. [43]He trusts in God; let God deliver him now, if he desires him; for he said, "I am the Son of God"'. [44]And the robbers who were crucified with him also reviled him in the same way.

Matthew 27.38—44 (RSV)

You are looking at a piece of wasteland. No one wants it. Nothing will grow there. No one will buy it. No building could be erected there — it is too mis-shapen. It looks like a man's skull, bare and boney. But it possesses two assets: it is elevated and public, and thus serves as the ideal place for crucifixions. Sticking up gaunt it makes a repulsive platform, and being hard by the roadway into the city an audience constantly coming and going is assured. This is the place to which the Roman execution squad marched Jesus. They had been there before and they had perfected the drill. Business-like, they nailed up Jesus first, then the other two. Three crosses in all; Jesus in the middle. So the macabre stage was set and the watchers settled down. There was to be gloating entertainment for several hours, and the weather was fine.

Look at the onlookers. St Matthew would have us observe two groups; the chance passers-by whether for business or for pleasure, making their passing comments; and the members of the religious establishment, clearly recognizable, who had established themselves at the place for the business and the wry pleasure of mocking, both groups voicing the identical derisions — 'he can't come down from his cross'; 'he is powerless'; 'he saved others but cannot save himself'. And the two other victims, who were anything but mere onlookers, nevertheless joined in with the same ribaldry. It is precisely here, then, we are to discover what the crucifixion of Christ is about — his power and his powerlessness, that is the paradox of his power.

Suppose Jesus had come down from the cross. Suppose the nails had miraculously lifted themselves out of their sockets in the wood; suppose the wound-marks had suddenly been obliterated, suppose that ridiculous crown of thorns had in a moment been transformed into a royal diadem and that Jesus had descended majestically into the circle upon circle of gasping watchers at the foot of his torture stake, the stage and auditorium on Skull hill resounding with shouts of victory; and there, crawling in the dust was Caiaphas, confessing his guilt, and Pilate his cowardly condemnation of an innocent victim. Would Jesus have been our redeemer if this had happened? Would he not have been a browbeater of us into mental submission? There would be nothing left for us but to cave in to his uncanny power, no room at all for the response of our freewill, and no place, therefore, for adoration — we would have been crushed by the spectacular.

Let us go back to his baptism in the River Jordan, back to the Spirit's driving him into the wilderness, back to those forty days and forty nights when he walked up and down agonizing over how he was to conduct his ministry. And the devil came to him suggesting that he buy the populace with bread and dazzle the people with wonders as if he were a magician, *but he refused*. He would not be a tyrant cheating them of their faculties of judgement. Always room would be left for people to choose. Belief or unbelief must be left as open possibilities. He would not wield his power to crush our human freedom.

'Come down from the cross that we may see and believe', cried the mocking passers-by and priests and lawyers. But the truth is that had he done so they would have known, and we would have known, that Jesus of Nazareth was not the Son of God. The proper picture of God, the true revelation of God, is not one of naked power but one of love, and love can be accepted or refused; it does not compel.

Of course the crucifixion was horrible. All crucifixions were horrible and they were not rare. All their victims suffered as terribly as Jesus, some with courage and defiance. Not in its intensity was Christ's passion unique but in his will to undergo it; his nailing to the cross with common criminals *was his ministry* which he would neither avoid, escape or tone down. His refusal to descend from it, whatever the mocking, was and is his revelation of what God is like.

*   *   *

And now intellectualizing runs out. It can take us no further. There is nothing more to say but as we move nearer to the exit of the art gallery of the gospels with this picture of three crosses in line, and Jesus in the midst, we recall how in the face of some calamity in our world we have cried out, 'Why doesn't God do something, something staggering to show he is there?' The answer is on that central cross: he did not come down because he was God incarnate.

Prayer

> Hold thou thy cross before my closing eyes;
> Shine through the gloom, and point me to the skies:
> Heaven's morning breaks, and earth's vain shadows flee;
> In life, in death, O Lord, abide with me.

H.F. Lyte

The evidence of the empty tomb

20 Now on the first day of the week Mary Magdalene came to the tomb early, while it was still dark, and saw that the stone had been taken away from the tomb. ²So she ran, and went to Simon Peter and the other disciple, the one whom Jesus loved, and said to them, 'They have taken the Lord out of the tomb, and we do not know where they have laid him'. ³Peter then came out with the other disciple, and they went toward the tomb. ⁴They both ran, but the other disciple outran Peter and reached the tomb first; ⁵and stooping to look in, he saw the linen cloths lying there, but he did not go in. ⁶Then Simon Peter came, following him, and went into the tomb; he saw the linen cloths lying, ⁷and the napkin, which had been on his head, not lying with the linen cloths but rolled up in a place by itself. ⁸Then the other disciple, who reached the tomb first, also went in, and he saw and believed; ⁹for as yet they did not know the scripture, that he must rise from the dead. ¹⁰Then the disciples went back to their homes.

John 20.1—10 (RSV)

We are looking at three people — Mary Magdalene, Peter and the 'other disciple', most likely John — each with different aspirations and private sorrows but bound together by their common loss of Jesus. Let us imagine for a moment the individual patterns of this picture.

If Mary Magdalene slept that night it could only have been fitfully. The light of her life had gone out. Nothing remained for her now but brokenness. He on whom she had poured out her grateful devotion was dead and buried. She had seen him die. She had seen where he was buried. She would haunt the place. To her it was sacred. So the merest chink of morning light saw her up and about, creeping along the deserted streets out through the city gate, and on to the garden where all that made life for her lay entombed. On arriving she stood back, aghast: the great stone rolled over the entrance had been removed. She turned and ran first to Peter's lodging, then to John's, breathlessly conveying her deduction from what she had seen — the precious Lord's body had been stolen and hidden.

The two men did not wait to discuss anything, they both ran, each as fast as he could. John outstripped Peter to arrive first at the tomb's entrance standing wide open. He stooped to peep inside and found himself staring at linen burial clothes; only linen burial clothes. Then Peter arrived panting. Impulsively as ever he went straight in. What he saw was the winding burial sheet for the Lord's body, not in a rumpled pile, but still retaining the shape of the body, though flattened. Some inches away, where the neck and face had been left unswathed according to burial custom, lay the linen head-piece still neatly rolled and retaining the shape of the head. Bewildered, he stood there. The tomb could not have been rifled. Thieves would not take the body and leave the costly winding sheets. Then John entered. He saw what Peter saw but with insight: the Lord's physical body clearly was no more, not because some-one had stolen it but because it had become a spiritual presence. What he was looking at in the empty tomb was evidence for him of resurrection to an altogether different life. All along in his close companionship with Jesus he had felt at times almost overcome by how different he was. This was no mere man, yet a real man he was. Now, standing there in that empty tomb he knew — Jesus was the Lord now risen from the dead.

★　　★　　★

As we stand with this picture before us, do we see the risen Christ, or do we scrutinize the facts desperately seeking for some concrete evidence or tangible proof of his resurrection? We are all different: the three figures in this picture each has different reactions to the empty tomb. But John was the first one to apprehend and believe in the resurrection of Jesus. What is more, he came to this faith with-out any appearance to him of the risen Christ. All he had was the evidence of the empty tomb and the depth of his devotion to Jesus. And he was not only the first to believe in the resurrection, he was the first in that long line of believers who have believed *without* an appearance to them of the risen Christ. We cannot all be like John: some of us need more reassurance than others. But we cannot demand absolute proof on our terms. We have the scriptures including this account at which we have been looking, we have the Holy Spirit to teach us, and we have the faith of the Church which has survived many onslaughts. Yes, we have grounds for belief in the resurrection of Jesus. We can know spiritually the risen Christ; we can know 'the power of his resurrection' now.

85

Prayer

'On the third day he rose again
    according to the scriptures.'
Yes, Lord, we repeat it every Sunday.
    We say we believe it
    and in a way we do believe it.
We believe it because the Church believes it,
    always has believed it;
    though we cannot prove the resurrection —
    no one can.
Yet without it our faith is empty:
    empty of power,
    empty of hope.
Enliven our faith, Lord.
Let the world see that our church
    is the Church of the resurrection,
    pulsating with life,
    strong in consolation,
    active in ministry,
    especially to the needy in body, mind and spirit.
We pray in the name of our risen and exalted Lord
    Jesus Christ, the Saviour.

Makeshift rescue

[39]Now when it was day, they did not recognize the land, but they noticed a bay with a beach, on which they planned if possible to bring the ship ashore. [40]So they cast off the anchors and left them in the sea, at the same time loosening the ropes that tied the rudders; then hoisting the foresail to the wind they made for the beach. [41]But striking a shoal they ran the vessel aground; the bow stuck and remained immovable, and the stern was broken up by the surf. [42]The soldiers' plan was to kill the prisoners, lest any should swim away and escape; [43]but the centurion, wishing to save Paul, kept them from carrying out their purpose. He ordered those who could swim to throw them-

selves overboard first and make for the land, ⁴⁴and the rest on planks
or on pieces of the ship. And so it was that all escaped to land.

Acts 27.39—44 (RSV)

This shipwreck scene calls to mind Gericault's painting in the
Louvre entitled *The Raft of Medusa* and the sensation it caused
when first exhibited because the artist sought to depict realism in
life over and against the insipid romanticism which dominated so
much of the art of his time (1791—1824). The shipwreck scene of
Acts 27 which St Luke painted is likewise realistic, and presumably
so because he, the artist, was there. With the other marooned passengers he escaped to the shore as best he could. There is no miracle
in this picture; nothing like St Mark's picture of Jesus in the
storm-tossed boat on the lake of Galilee calling 'Peace be still' and
'the wind ceased and there was a great calm' (Mark 4.39). The
furore of the storm never ceased to lash the grounded ship, breaking up its stern, till it had spent its force. The crew and passengers,
including both Paul and Luke, survived through their own efforts
at swimming, or by grabbing hold of floating planks of wood and
other bits of the stricken vessel. God did not intervene. There was
no miracle.

Maybe we disapprove of this realism. We reckon the Bible pictures ought always to show God intervening in life. God does
intervene: there are miracles recorded in the Bible, and if we insist
on erasing them all on the general ground that miracles do not happen we have divested the Bible of its *religious* value. What we seek
through religion is contact with a Power beyond the ordinary,
otherwise it has little point. Even so, in the Bible, and in life, miracles are rare. Special providences are rare and when they do occur
they are to be read as signs that God is present in and through the
regular operation of nature which after all is his creation. God was
not absent when the storm broke up the ship on which St Paul was
travelling. We may believe that it was God's purpose that his servant should arrive safely in Rome, but not by delivering him *from*
the storms of life, but rather *through* them, maybe in a desperate,
makeshift manner, perhaps clinging to a broken spar, if he could
not swim. There is miracle in the Bible but also realism. It is not a
'fantastic book'.

Given the option, most of us would arrange life to consist of a
stately cruise across untroubled waters in the full sunshine. But we

87

are not given the option, and rarely, if ever, is this the experience of humanity. Storms blow up, the sea turns rough, and there is even the fear of sinking altogether. Then there are frantic struggles to keep afloat, desperate efforts to grab hold of something which appears buoyant in the turbulent waters. So it is that large numbers of people turn to religion, not openly, not consistently, but urgently in the secret places of their hearts and minds. Faced with calamity, they clutch at a prayer; broken by bereavement, they recall snatches of some half-forgotten hymn or verse of scripture which seems to say that death is not the end; when doubt gnaws at what they had taken to be eternal truth they hold on to the fact that some man, some woman, whom they held in high regard believed, and this has to suffice for their own faith. All these struggles are makeshift, desperate affairs, but they actually save people from drowning in the sea of their troubles and enable them to reach a place of safety, soaked no doubt to the skin, cold and miserable; but they have survived the storm that has broken over their life.

*   *   *

Perhaps, if we were open and honest, many of us who profess to be Christians would have to admit how humble has been the means by which we have come to our own faith. We would like to persuade ourselves that calmly and rationally, perhaps even philosophically, we weighed up the pros and cons of Christian belief and unbelief, and in the maturity of our judgement we 'opted for' faith. But, for the vast majority of us, this self-satisfying approach did not take place. We are Christians because we found ourselves members of a Christian family, or were attracted by a Christian teacher or clergy-man, or felt at home in some club or community, or we drifted into some evangelistic campaign, or we went forward for confirmation because some of our friends went forward and we did not wish to be left out. Hardly very high flown any of it! But we landed some-how in the lifeboat of the Christian faith. Two lessons follow from this. We should never be ashamed of the humble means by which we, or other Christians, have come to their faith; and we should never try to snatch away the humble makeshift bits of religious wood by which any man or woman has managed to keep afloat in the contemporary sea of unbelief.

Prayer

Lord, this is a rough world;
    the twentieth century has been rough;
        rough in Europe,
        rough in the Middle East,
        rough in Africa.
    Look which way we will
    there has been cruelty,
        bloodshed,
        oppression,
        hunger.
    And our own small worlds
    have experienced storms,
        through illness,
        through bereavement,
        through redundancies
        and the consequences of the rising
            cost of living.
At times we have been afraid, terribly afraid.
    Save us, Lord, we ask you,
        if not out of our troubles,
        then through our troubles.
    By whatever means there may be,
    let the life-line of faith be thrown to us
    so that we may make for firm ground
    and begin life afresh.
We ask in the name of our Lord, Jesus Christ.

Self-giving love

13 Though I speak with the tongues of men and of angels, and have not charity, I am become as sounding brass, or a tinkling cymbal.

²And though I have the gift of prophecy, and understand all mysteries, and all knowledge; and though I have all faith, so that I could remove mountains, and have not charity, I am nothing.

³And though I bestow all my goods to feed the poor, and though I give my body to be burned, and have not charity, it profiteth me nothing.

⁴Charity suffereth long, and is kind; charity envieth not; charity vaunteth not itself, is not puffed up,

⁵Doth not behave itself unseemly, seeketh not her own, is not easily provoked, thinketh no evil;

⁶Rejoiceth not in iniquity, but rejoiceth in the truth;

⁷Beareth all things, believeth all things, hopeth all things, endureth all things.

⁸Charity never faileth: but whether there be prophecies, they shall fail; whether there be tongues, they shall cease; whether there be knowledge, it shall vanish away.

⁹For we know in part, and we prophesy in part.

¹⁰But when that which is perfect is come, then that which is in part shall be done away.

¹¹When I was a child, I spake as a child, I understood as a child, I thought as a child; but when I became a man, I put away childish things.

¹²For now we see through a glass, darkly; but then face to face: now I know in part; but then shall I know even as also I am known.

¹³And now abideth faith, hope, charity, these three; but the greatest of these is charity.

1 Corinthians 13 (AV)

Although this passage of the Bible does not present us with an action picture as do most of the others considered in this book, it is not possible to omit it from a collection of biblical masterpieces. It represents an inspired outburst of St Paul concerning self-giving love which was provoked by the situation he saw among the Christians in Corinth where he had established a church. It must be one of the most well-known chapters in the Bible but we shall not be able to appreciate it unless we picture the situation where it originated.

Corinth was a busy, bustling, even brash, cosmopolitan city which derived its significance primarily from its location on one of the great trading routes between East and West of the Roman Empire. It seemed everybody of any significance at one time or another passed through Corinth, even if they did not stay there. No one could call the place refined or exclusive; it was inclusive of all that was pushing, vulgar and noisy. It could be described as the most immoral city in the Roman Empire dedicated as it was to Aphrodite, the goddess of sensual lust. But it was energetic, intellectually as well as in commerce, and, with it all, encouraged a great love of talking. St Paul nourished a church there, a lively church but one that caused him much trouble. He wrote at least four letters to it, two of which are included in our New Testament. Apart from acts of flagrant sexual immorality on the part of some members of the church, the quarrelling, and the arguing, there was a genuine growth of spiritual life, but even here there was a tendency towards showiness. The idea of spiritual gifts was especially attractive to the Corinthians, appealing to their sense of the dramatic. How exciting to be able to hold forth 'in a tongue', evidence of spiritual superiority (so they thought)! How thrilling to be able to confound the regular medics by exercising the gift of physical healing for incurable illnesses. Clearly there was a kind of glory to be obtained from the Christian gospel. And as St Paul sat in Ephesus about the year AD 56 brooding on this strange mixture of spiritual vitality and self-centredness in the church of Corinth, there issued from his sensitive and quivering spirit this striking hymn to love: not *'eros'*, be it noted, not self-centred love, not grasping love and certainly not lust, but *'agape'*, self-giving love, self-sacrificing love, a word representing a lifestyle the church in Corinth had to learn, and all churches everywhere since have had to learn if they are to exhibit the genuine Christian character. *'Agape'* has been translated as 'charity' in the Authorised Version of the Bible and conveys the gentle, giving nature of this distinctively Christian virtue.

In the hymn Paul shows attention to the characteristics of love as seen in action, the duration of love into eternity, and he also stresses the futility of all other spiritual gifts in the absence of love. All the 'trimmings' of Christianity which proved so attractive to the Corinthian church were utterly meaningless without *agape*, charity or selfless love.

★　　★　　★

In a holiday home in Germany the visitors were so attracted by a meditation framed and hanging on one of the walls entitled *Without Love* that many of them copied down the words although the name of the author was unknown. Translated into English it reads:

91

Care without love makes for peevishness.
Responsibility without love makes for dogmatism.
Righteousness without love makes for hardness.
Cleverness without love makes for cunning.
Friendliness without love makes for hypocrisy.
Order without love makes for pettiness.
Honour without love makes for pride.
Possession without love makes for meanness.
Faith without love makes for fanaticism.
A life without love is senseless.

From the Neukirchener Kalender, 31 January 1989

We know that love can so easily be distorted by the self-centredness of our own desires. Sometimes we may be only too aware of our continual failing to live up to the self-giving ministry of Christ. But often we may be totally blind to the way in which we 'administer' our love on 'certain conditions'. St Paul's picture of love captures truth, perhaps unattainable for most of us with our human failings, but, nevertheless, the ideal upon which we may set our sights.

Prayer

O Lord, who hast taught us that all our doings without charity are nothing worth: send thy Holy Ghost, and pour into our hearts that most excellent gift of charity, the very bond of peace and of all virtues, without which whosoever liveth is counted dead before thee: grant this for thine only Son Jesus Christ's sake. Amen.

From the Book of Common Prayer

A new song

¹¹Then I looked, and I heard around the throne and the living creatures and the elders the voice of many angels, numbering myriads of myriads and thousands of thousands, ¹²saying with a loud voice, 'Worthy is the Lamb who was slain, to receive power and wealth and wisdom and might and honour and glory and blessing!' ¹³And I heard every creature in heaven and on earth and under the earth and in the sea, and all therein, saying, 'To him who sits upon the throne and to the Lamb be blessing and honour and glory and might for ever and ever!' ¹⁴And the four living creatures said, 'Amen!' and the elders fell down and worshipped.

Revelation 5.11—14 (RSV)

These verses stand in the book of Revelation as an awe-inspiring climax to Chapters 4 and 5. In those chapters dramatic tension is raised almost to breaking point by a vision of God on his throne holding in his right hand a closed book sealed tight with seven seals. It is the closed book of human history, past, present and future. And it remains closed; no one can open it or peer inside and read it, although every man and woman aches to look into the future — their own future and the world's future. The Seer's heart, too, failed with grief that no one could be found worthy to unlock the secrets of what is to be. But at last there came a message: the Lion of the tribe of Judah was to open the book. A lion, however, is not what the Seer saw but a lamb standing as though it had been slain yet standing alive, indeed alive for evermore. So gentleness, not force, was to be the way of conquest. At which point the words of a new song are sung, 'Worthy art thou to take the scroll and to open its seals', new because there is a new theme — the theme of redemption.

All this is preliminary to the five verses in the picture before us; and to this preliminary is another preliminary, indeed Chapters 4 and 5 of the Book of Revelation, ending with these five verses, are to be read together: they spell out the two essential themes of the Christian gospel, namely creation (Chapter 4) and redemption (Chapter 5). The Christian gospel is not only the good news of the world's redemption, it is also the good news of the world's creation.

The world is God's and when he redeems it through Christ, he redeems what is his own. We cannot disregard the created order or exploit it as if it were the property of human beings to do with as they like.

This canvas is bursting with colour and life. It is an inspiring celebration of the supreme power and loving nature of God controlling, sustaining and restoring his world. What, however, stands out in this scene beyond all else is the Lamb that had been slain, that is Christ the redeemer seated on the throne with God the Creator. It is astonishing that a Jew has arrived at this conviction. But what more striking evidence is there of the place assigned to Jesus even before the end of the first century? — God *and* *Christ* on the throne and worshipped together.

So we reach the grand climax, the eternal throne of God and a throng surrounding it too great to be numbered chanting with a loud voice, 'Worthy is the Lamb who was slain', worthy indeed to receive a mighty sevenfold acclaim which we can now scarcely read without hearing in our minds the triumphant bursts of praise in the music of Handel's glorious oratorio *Messiah*, catching surely forever the magnificence of this biblical masterpiece. Nor is this all; not content with describing the living creatures, the elders and the many angels lifting up their voices, the artist paints the whole of creation into his picture — 'every creature in heaven and on earth and under the earth and in the sea, and all therein, saying, "To him who sits upon the throne and to the Lamb be blessing and honour and glory and might for ever and ever!"' Then comes the giant roar of the 'Amen' and the equally shattering silence which followed as all fell down to worship.

★ ★ ★

What more eloquent testimony than this could there possibly be to the majesty of the gospel of our creation and redemption and the centrality of the crucified and risen Lord who holds the key of all our futures? It is a masterpiece.

Prayer

> We praise thee, O God: we acknowledge thee
> to be the Lord.

All the earth doth worship thee: the Father
    everlasting . . .
The holy Church throughout all the world:
    doth acknowledge thee;
The Father of an infinite Majesty;
Thine honourable, true and only Son;
Also the Holy Ghost the Comforter.
Thou art the King of glory O Christ.
Thou art the everlasting Son of the Father.
When thou tookest upon thee to deliver man
    thou didst not abhor the Virgin's womb.
When thou hadst overcome the sharpness of death
    thou didst open the kingdom of heaven to all believers.
Thou sittest at the right hand of God in the glory
of the Father . . .
O Lord, save thy people and bless thine heritage . . .
O Lord, in thee have I trusted
    let me never be confounded.

From the Te Deum, Book of Common Prayer